Social Studies Alive!™
Regions of Our Country

Teachers' Curriculum Institute

Bert Bower   Jim Lobdell

Managing Editor: Laura Alavosus
Production Editor: Mali Apple
Editorial Assistant: Anna Embree
Art Director: Tim Stephenson
Production Coordinator: Lynn Sanchez
Senior Graphic Designer: Chrisy Uyeno
Graphic Designers: Katy Haun, Victoria Philp,
    Paul Rebello
Photographer: Tim Stephenson
Photo Acquisitions: Anna Embree
Audio Director: Katy Haun
Operations Manager: Ellen Mapstone

This book is published by Teachers' Curriculum Institute.

Teachers' Curriculum Institute
PO Box 50996
1170 East Meadow Drive
Palo Alto, CA 94303

Customer Service: 800-497-6138
www.historyalive.com

ISBN 1-58371-326-3

1 2 3 4 5 6 7 8 9 10 07 06 05 04 03 02

Program Directors

Bert Bower

Jim Lobdell

Program Author

Vicki LaBoskey, Professor of Education,
Mills College, Oakland, California
Ph.D., Curriculum and Teacher Education,
Stanford University, Stanford, California

Student Edition Author

Diane Hart, Social Studies Specialist
M.A., History, Stanford University,
Stanford, California

Senior Curriculum Developer

Steve Seely

Contributing Curriculum Developers

Joyce Bartky

Anne Maloney

Elizabeth Sarica

Kelly Shafsky

Reading Specialist

Barbara Schubert, Reading Specialist,
Saint Mary's College, Moraga, California
Ph.D., Education, University of California,
Santa Barbara, California

Teacher Consultants

Jane Crowe
Brookwood Elementary School,
Tuscaloosa County, Alabama

Khieta Davis
Flower City School #54,
Rochester, New York

Ann Dawson, Educational Consultant,
Intermediate Curriculum Specialist
Gahanna, Ohio

Elizabeth McKenna
St. Thomas Aquinas Catholic School,
Orlando Diocese, Florida

Geography Specialist

David Knipfer
Mapping Specialists, Ltd.
Madison, Wisconsin

Internet Consultant

Chuck Taft
University School of Milwaukee,
Milwaukee, Wisconsin

Contents

chapter 1

What Are the Social Sciences?

1.1 Introduction

Why are some people rich and others poor? How can studying the past help us live better today? These are the kinds of questions **social scientists** ask.

The **social sciences** are the study of how people live in groups. Some social scientists study small groups, such as families. Others study large groups, such as nations. They learn about the economy, geography, history, and politics of the groups they study.

Social scientists want to understand why people behave as they do. To find out, they watch people. They ask questions. They study written records, such as letters and news stories.

They also study artifacts. Artifacts are things people use in their daily lives. Your clothes are a kind of artifact. So are all the things in your backpack. What would a social scientist learn about you by studying these artifacts? You might be surprised by the answer!

Social Scientists

Economist

Historian

Geographer

Political Scientist

Rising prices are one way to measure the economy.

1.2 The Social Science of Economics

You find a dollar in your pocket. Should you spend it on a snack? Save it for a new comic book? You might think no one cares how you choose to spend your money. Not true! Some social scientists are **economists**. They are very interested in the choices people make every day.

Economists study the **economy** of a city, state, or country. An economy is the way people in a community use resources to meet their wants and needs. We all need food, clothing, and shelter. We all have things we want but don't really need. You may want a new game. Your parents may want a new car. In the economy of the United States, a variety of resources meets people's needs and wants.

Economics is the study of how people make, buy, and sell things. Economists want to know how people decide what to make. They also want to know how people decide what to buy.

Imagine that you are an economist. You are studying how families decide what to buy. What artifacts might help you? Here are a few ideas:

- price tags
- sales slips
- coupons
- advertisements
- things your family bought recently

economist a social scientist who studies the economy of a community
economy the way people in a community use resources to meet their needs and wants

1.3 The Social Science of Geography

You are on a trip somewhere new. Nothing looks familiar. You begin to feel a little lost. Finally, you ask yourself, "Where am I?"

You could use some help from another social scientist, a **geographer**. Geographers like to know where places are on a map. They study Earth's surface to find out what lies around them.

geographer a social scientist who studies the natural and constructed features of Earth's surface

Geographers use maps and globes to show the features of our planet's surface. Land, water, plants, and animals are made by nature. These are called *natural features*. People build towns, roads, bridges, and dams. These are called *constructed features*.

The United States has just about every natural and constructed feature on Earth. It has mountains, deserts, rivers, and lakes. It has large cities filled with people. It has tiny towns. It also has vast empty spaces.

Pretend you are a geographer. You are studying the natural and constructed features of your town. These artifacts might help you:

- maps
- weather records
- newspaper articles
- wildflowers
- birds' nests

Learning to use maps is an important part of thinking like a geographer.

1.4 The Social Science of Political Science

You are riding your bike down the street when *bam!* your front wheel hits a pothole. You go flying over the handlebars. As you pick yourself up, you grumble, "This is dangerous! Who's in charge of fixing the streets, anyway?"

This is just the kind of question a **political scientist** might ask. Political scientists are interested in who is in charge. They want to know how people get the power to run a city, state, or nation. They also look at how the people in charge use their power.

Political science is the study of governments. All groups—even families—have some sort of government. A government is a system for deciding what is best for the group. Its main job is to make and carry out rules and laws. These rules help people live together in peace. Governments also supply things that people need. Your local government provides things that you need, such as schools and safe streets.

Imagine that a political scientist is visiting your home. What artifacts might interest him or her? Here are a few ideas:

- legal forms
- election ads
- stories about government
- voter information
- newspaper articles about laws

Protest signs such as these are one way that people tell the government what they want and need.

political scientist a social scientist who studies government

1.5 The Social Science of History

You take a wrong turn one day and find yourself in a cemetery. It seems creepy at first. But then you start reading the tombstones. You see several old stones from the 1800s. Some mark the graves of babies. "Why did so many babies die so young?" you wonder. Now you are thinking like a **historian**.

History is the study of the past. Human beings have been around a very long time. As a result, we have a lot of past to study. Historians, however, are most interested in the last few thousand years of human history. This is when people began leaving written records.

historian a social scientist who studies the past

The first question historians ask is, *What happened in the past?* To find out, they study all kinds of records and artifacts. Once historians know what happened, they ask other questions, such as: *Who took part in these events? How did these things happen? And why did they happen this way?*

Imagine that you have been asked to write a history of your family. What kinds of artifacts and records would help you? Here are some suggestions:

- birth certificates
- baby books
- family photos
- letters
- diaries
- family treasures

This old school photograph is an artifact a historian might like.

1.6 Thinking Like a Social Scientist

Now that you know more about social scientists, can you start thinking like one?

Try this experiment. Choose one object from your desk or backpack to study. Ask yourself, *What kind of social scientists would be most interested in this artifact? An economist? A geographer? A political scientist? A historian? What would that person want to know about this artifact? Who made it? How much it cost? Where it came from? Something else?*

One group of fourth graders tried this experiment with a pair of shoes. To their surprise, the shoe turned out to be a pretty interesting artifact. Here are their results.

An economist would want to know such things as:

1. How much did the shoes cost to make?
2. How much did you pay for them?
3. Why did you choose to buy these shoes instead of another pair of shoes?

A geographer would ask:

1. Where were these shoes made?
2. What resources were used to make them?
3. How did they travel from the factory to your shoe store?

A political scientist might ask:

1. Who was in charge of buying this pair of shoes?
2. How did they decide which shoes to buy? Did they buy the best quality shoes? The cheapest shoes? Or the shoes they wanted most?

A historian might ask:

1. How have shoes changed over time?
2. What is the history of these shoes? When were they made? Who made them? Why did they make them? What has happened to these shoes since they were made?

1.7 Looking Ahead

You are about to begin a tour through the United States. Along the way, you will meet five social scientists. They will be your tour guides to different parts of our country. They have chosen places to visit that they hope you will like.

You don't need to pack a suitcase for your trip. But you do need to pack your brain with some useful information. You'll find what you need to know in the next two chapters.

In Chapter 2, you will look at the geography of our country. You will learn some geography terms that your guides will use. You will also learn about some of our country's most important natural features. You will hear more about these features on your tours.

In Chapter 3, you will read about the history of the American people. You will meet five groups of people who came to live in America. You will find out what brought them to this land. You'll also learn how they have made our country a better place.

Once you begin your tour, don't forget to think like a social scientist. Ask lots of good questions. But most of all, have a good time!

chapter 2

Exploring Regions of the United States

2.1 Introduction

Because Earth is so large, geographers divide it into regions to study. A region is an area with common features that set it apart from other areas. In this book, we have divided the United States into five regions to study.

In this chapter, you will learn how geographers study regions. One way is by using maps. Geographers use maps to help them think about five topics, or themes, of geography. These are the five themes of geography:

Location: Where is the place located? What is it near?

Place: What is this place like?

Human-environmental interaction: How does this place affect the people living here? And how do the people who live here affect this place?

Movement: How do people, goods, and ideas move to and from this place?

Regions: What features about this place set it apart from other places?

Try answering the questions above about a place you know well—your school. Now you are thinking like a geographer. Keep thinking that way as you read more about the regions of the United States.

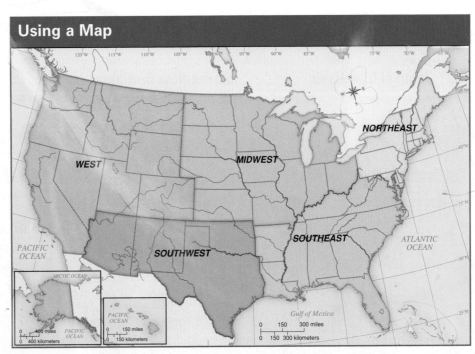

Using a Map

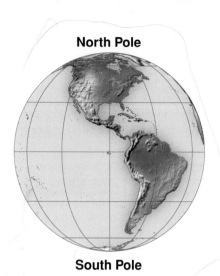

North Pole

South Pole

2.2 Location and Direction

Every place has its own location. A location is the site where something can be found. People describe locations in many ways. You might describe the location of your home by talking about what it is near. Or you might use your street address.

Geographers use globes and maps to show the locations of places on Earth. Globes are round like our Earth. They are useful when you want to know where places are on the planet. When you need to see where many places are all at once, maps can be more useful. Maps show all or part of Earth on a flat surface.

To use a map, you need to know the four cardinal directions. North is the direction toward the North Pole. When you face north, your back is facing south. East is to your right. West is to your left. On a map, the letters *N, S, E,* and *W* stand for the cardinal directions.

The intermediate directions are halfway between the cardinal directions. Northeast, for example, lies halfway between north and east. The other intermediate directions are southeast, southwest, and northwest. On a map, the letters *NE, SE, SW,* and *NW* stand for the intermediate directions.

Most maps use a compass rose to show directions.

Cardinal Directions

Intermediate Directions

Compass Rose

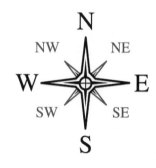

2.3 Scales and Symbols

Maps never show sizes and distances as they really are. They are always much smaller than the part of Earth they represent. A short distance on a map stands for a much greater distance on Earth.

The **scale** of a map shows the relationship between map distances and real distances. A map's scale can be shown in many ways. The most common is a line scale. The map on this page has two line scales. One is for miles, and the other is for kilometers. The mile scale line shows that 1 inch on the map equals 100 miles on Earth.

Maps use symbols to show other kinds of information. A symbol is anything that stands for something else. Sometimes symbols look like what they stand for. For example, mapmakers often use tiny airplanes to stand for airports.

Color is another important map symbol. The color blue usually stands for water. Mapmakers often use different colors to show separate states or countries.

Mapmakers use a map key to explain their symbols. The **map key** tells what each symbol stands for. Look at the map on this page. What does the star stand for?

scale a diagram that explains distances on a map

map key an explanation of what the symbols on a map stand for

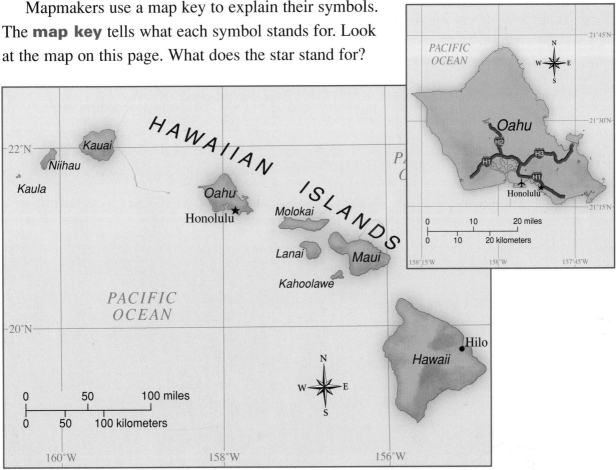

2.4 Lines of Latitude

Suppose you wanted to describe the exact location of a place on Earth. To help you do this, mapmakers invented a system of imaginary lines around the globe. Some of these lines run east and west around the globe. They are called lines of latitude. **Lines of latitude** are also known as parallels. This is because they are always the same distance apart.

Lines of latitude tell us how far north or south of the equator a place is. The equator is a line of latitude. It divides Earth into two halves: the Northern Hemisphere and the Southern Hemisphere. Because the United States lies north of the equator, it is in the Northern Hemisphere.

The equator is the starting point for measuring latitude. It is labeled 0°, or zero degrees. Parallels north of the equator are labeled *N*. The North Pole is 90°N. Parallels south of the equator are labeled *S*. The South Pole is 90°S.

Lines of latitude measure between 0° and 90°N or 90°S. The closer a parallel is to the equator, the smaller its number of degrees. The closer it is to one of the poles, the greater its number of degrees.

lines of latitude
imaginary lines around the globe that run east and west; also called *parallels*

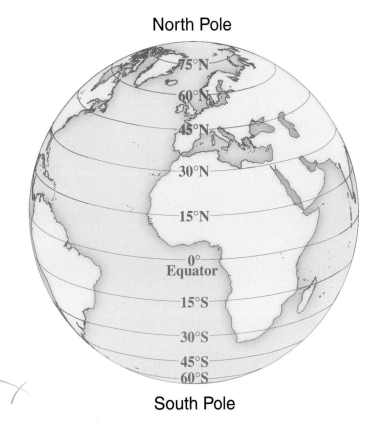

North Pole

75°N
60°N
45°N
30°N
15°N
0°
Equator
15°S
30°S
45°S
60°S

South Pole

2.5 Lines of Longitude

Lines of longitude tell us how far to the east or west we need to go to locate a place. Look at the map on this page. It shows lines of longitude circling Earth. These lines are also called *meridians*.

Unlike lines of latitude, meridians are not parallel to each other. All meridians meet at the North Pole and the South Pole. The distance between meridians is greatest at the equator. That distance shrinks as you move from the equator to the poles.

Can you find the line on the map that is labeled *prime meridian*? This imaginary line divides the world into the Eastern Hemisphere and the Western Hemisphere. Because the United States lies west of the prime meridian, it is in the Western Hemisphere.

The longitude of the prime meridian is 0°. Lines of longitude west of the prime meridian are labeled *W* for west. Meridians east of the prime meridian are labeled *E* for east.

Lines of longitude measure between 0° and 180°W or 180°E. The closer a meridian is to the prime meridian, the smaller its number of degrees. The farther it is from the prime meridian, the greater its number of degrees.

lines of longitude
imaginary lines around the globe that run between the North and South Poles; also called *meridians*

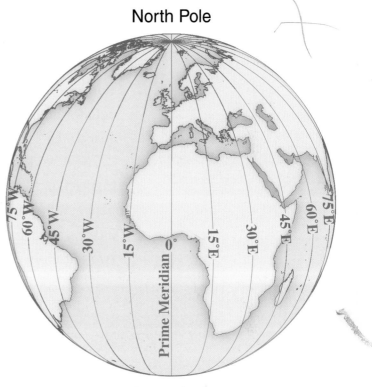

North Pole

South Pole

A boat's location on the ocean can be pinpointed using latitude and longitude.

2.6 The Global Grid

Mapmakers combine lines of longitude and latitude to form a grid. A grid is a set of crisscrossing lines. The grid you see is on the map below is called a **global grid** because it covers the whole Earth.

Using the lines of latitude and longitude on the global grid, you can locate places anywhere in the world. For example, suppose you want to locate New Orleans on the map below. It is 30 degrees north of the equator, or 30°N. It is also 90 degrees west of the prime meridian, or 90°W. When locating places on a map, latitude is stated first, then longitude. So, the location of New Orleans is 30°N, 90°W.

The city of Uíge, Angola, is located at 8°S, 15°E. To find this location, put your finger on the map where the equator and the prime meridian meet. Move your finger east to the 15°E meridian. So far, so good.

Now you have a problem. The 8°S parallel is not marked on this map. You know, though, that 8°S must lie between the equator and 15°S. If you move your finger along the 15°E meridian to the spot halfway between these two parallels, you will find the city you are looking for.

global grid the grid formed by crisscrossing lines of latitude and longitude on a map

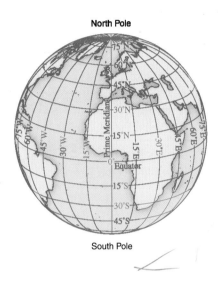

North Pole

South Pole

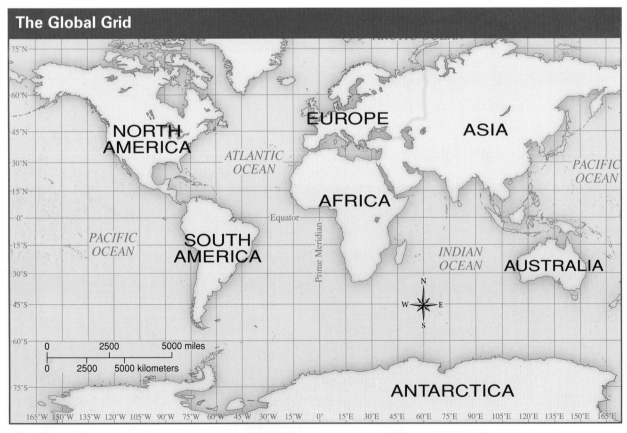

The Global Grid

2.7 Kinds of Maps

Geographers make different kinds of maps for different purposes. Maps that show natural features are called *physical maps*. A physical map shows landforms, such as mountains, valleys, and plains. Physical maps also show bodies of water, such as rivers, lakes, and oceans.

Other maps show humanmade features. For example, a political map shows cities, capitals, states, and countries. A road map shows roads and highwaysr. A historical map shows where events in the past took place.

Specialty maps show just one kind of information. Rainfall maps, for example, show how much rain falls in different parts of the world. Population maps show how many people live in different areas. Language maps show what languages people speak in different places.

The specialty map below is an elevation map of the United States. Elevation measures how high the land is above the ocean. The height of the ocean, or sea level, is zero elevation. The highest point in North America is Mount McKinley in Alaska. It rises 20,320 feet above sea level. What does the map show about your state's elevation?

specialty map a map that shows just one kind of information, such as rainfall or elevation

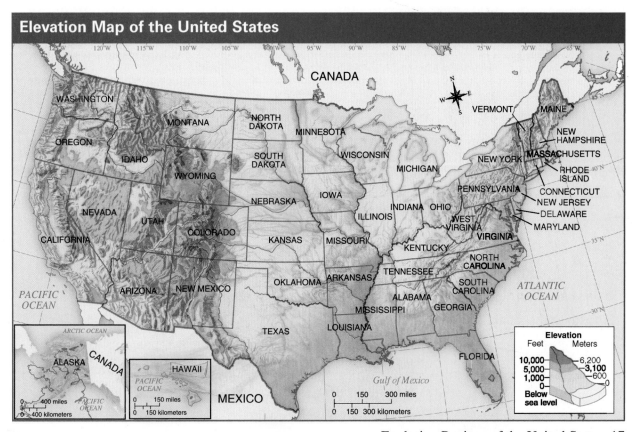

Elevation Map of the United States

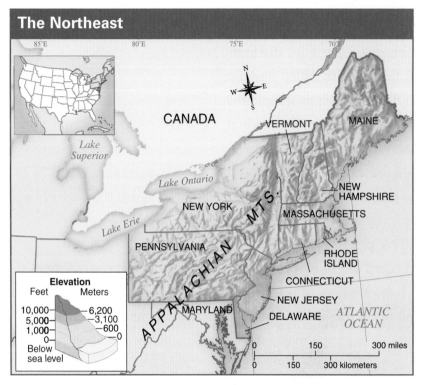

The Northeast

The Southeast

2.8 The Northeast and Southeast

The maps on this page show the Northeast and Southeast regions of the United States. These regions have much in common. Both lie beside the Atlantic Ocean. A low, flat plain runs along the coast in both regions. It is known as a **coastal plain**.

The Appalachian Mountains also run through both of these regions. Large rivers flow out of these mountains. The rivers that flow east cut across the coastal plain to the Atlantic Ocean. The rivers that flow west drain into the Gulf of Mexico.

While they are alike in some ways, the Northeast and Southeast regions have different climates. A place's climate is the kind of weather the place has over time. It includes temperature, rainfall, and wind conditions.

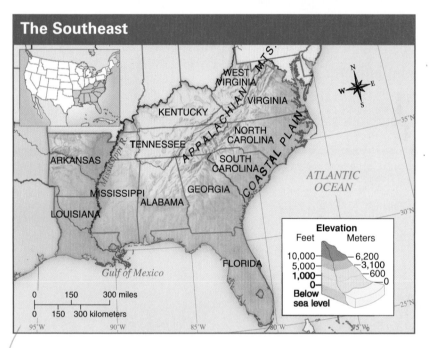

The Northeast region has a harsh climate. Winters there are long and cold. Snowstorms are common. Summers are warm but short compared to winters in the Southeast.

The Southeast region, in contrast, has a mild climate. Its winters are short and warm compared to those in the Northeast. Its summers are long, hot, and humid. Humid means damp or moist.

coastal plain low, flat land that runs along a coast

2.9 The Midwest and Southwest

The map on this page shows the Midwest and Southwest regions of the United States. These two regions lie at the center of our country.

The Midwest is an **inland** region. It does not border any ocean. However, the Great Lakes form part of the Midwest's northern border. These lakes are so large that they hold one fourth of all the freshwater in the world. This is enough to cover the United States with water 12 feet deep.

Most of the Midwest is flat plains. The Central Plains and Great Plains are covered with some of the best soil on Earth. That soil makes the Midwest an important farming region.

The Mississippi River runs through the Central Plains to the Gulf of Mexico. The Mississippi is the longest river in the United States. It is also a busy water highway for boats and barges.

Plains also cover the eastern part of the Southwest. Farther west, the land rises to form the Colorado Plateau. A **plateau** is a high, flat landform that rises steeply from the land around it.

Most of Colorado Plateau is fairly level. But it is crisscrossed by hundreds of deep canyons. The largest and most famous is the Grand Canyon.

inland an area of land that does not border an ocean

plateau a high, flat landform that rises steeply from the land around it

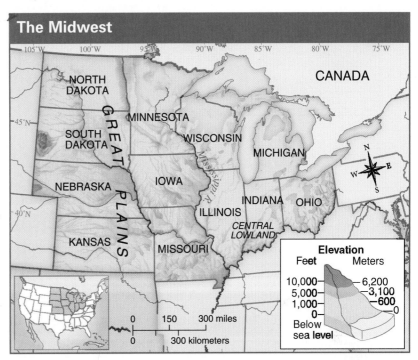

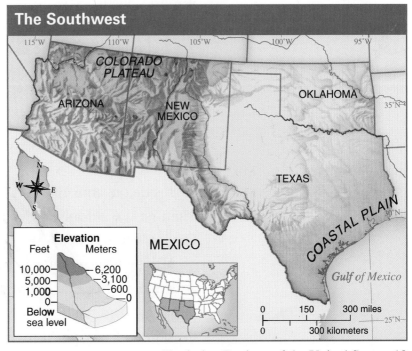

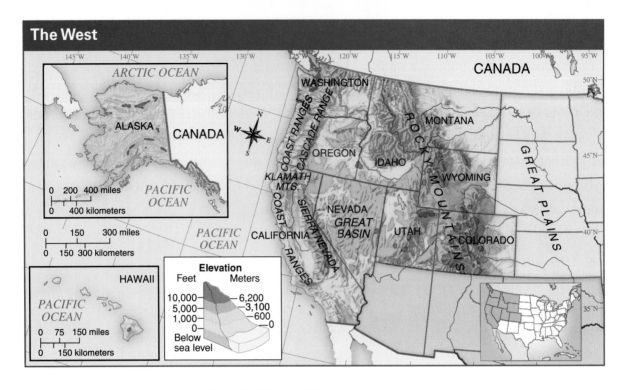

2.10 The West

Mountain ranges stretch across much of the West. The Rocky Mountains begin far to the north, in Alaska. From there they stretch south across Montana, Idaho, Wyoming, and Colorado.

The Great Basin lies to the west of the Rockies. A **basin** is a low, bowl-shaped landform that is lower than the land around it. Small ranges of hills line the Great Basin. On a map, they look like caterpillars crawling north toward Canada.

The mountain ranges along the Pacific Coast form a giant H on the map. The Coast Ranges make up the first long line of the H. These low hills seem to rise right out of the Pacific Ocean. The Sierra Nevada and Cascade Range form the second long line of the H. The Klamath Mountains form the crossbar. These mountains are covered with forests.

Inside the arms of the H lie two rich farming valleys. The first is California's Central Valley. The second is Oregon's Willamette Valley.

Hawaii is also mountainous. Its islands were made long ago by volcanoes. A volcano is an opening in Earth through which hot, melted rock and ash may pour out. As the liquid rock cools, it forms a cone-shaped mountain.

basin a bowl-shaped landform that is lower than the surrounding land

2.11 Chapter Summary

As you have just read, each region of the United States is different. Did you remember to think like a geographer as you looked at the maps of each region?

You now know that there are different kinds of maps. Some maps show locations of places around the world. Lines of latitude and longitude help us find places and measure distances north to south and east to west. Map scales also help us measure distances from place to place.

As you read about each region of the United States, you looked at physical maps. There are many other kinds of maps. To compare the weather around the country, you might use a climate map. A product map might show what each region grows or manufactures.

Each region also has its own history and culture. People in different regions eat different foods. They celebrate different holidays. They wear different kinds of clothing. And they honor different heroes.

Despite these differences, the five regions make up one nation. In the next chapter, you will learn more about the people of the United States.

chapter 3

The Peopling of the United States

3.1 Introduction

In the last chapter, you learned about the geography of the United States. But a nation is more than its land. A nation is a place where people live together under one government.

People in most nations are alike in many ways. They look alike. They speak the same language. They share the same culture, or way of life.

The United States is not like most nations. Americans are not all alike. Look around your school. Do the students you see all have the same color hair or skin? Do they all speak the same language at home? Do they all share the same culture? For many schools, the answer is no.

The United States is a **diverse** nation. This means that lots of different groups of people live in this country. In this chapter, you will meet five of those groups. And you will see how each group has made our country a better place to live.

Contributions to America

Native Americans formed groups. These groups developed their own languages and customs.

Native Americans
the first Americans

3.2 The First Americans Arrive

No one knows how people first came to the Americas. But scientists believe that they arrived long ago. At that time, Earth's climate was much colder than it is today. This long cold period is known as the ice age.

During the ice age, snow piled up in huge sheets of ice called *glaciers*. So much frozen water made the level of the oceans go down. A narrow strip of ocean between Asia and North America disappeared. This left a bridge of land between the two continents.

Scientists think that herds of animals wandered onto this land bridge looking for food. Hunters from Asia followed them. In time, they crossed the land bridge to North America. These hunters were probably the first Americans.

Just when the first Americans arrived is not known. We do know that over time they spread southward. Later the ocean washed over the land bridge again. By that time, people were living throughout North and South America. Today we know these people as **Native Americans**.

3.3 Contributions of Native Americans

Native Americans have affected American life in many ways. One great contribution has been their respect for nature. Native peoples used the land they lived on. But they seldom harmed it. They also named many of America's mountains, rivers, and states.

You may be able to see other contributions in your kitchen at home. Native Americans were the first to grow many of the foods we eat today. The two most popular foods they grew are corn and potatoes. They also grew such fruits and vegetables as beans, squash, and pineapples. They planted cocoa beans for making hot chocolate.

Here are still more Native American contributions to American life:

- *Holidays:* Thanksgiving, All-American Indian Days, Native American Day
- *Foods:* chocolate candy, potato chips, cranberry sauce, chewing gum, jerky
- *Words:* tepee, tomahawk, hammock, hurricane, skunk, tomato, avocado
- *Cool stuff:* moccasins, parkas, toboggans, pottery, jewelry, baskets, beadwork
- *Other gifts:* Indian pow-wows, legends, and myths; dogsleds

Squash and corn are just two of the vegetables first grown by Native Americans.

3.4 The Spanish Settle the Americas

In 1492, an explorer named Christopher Columbus left Spain in three small boats. Columbus believed that by sailing west across the Atlantic Ocean, he would reach Asia. Instead, he bumped into the Americas.

Columbus returned to Spain to tell about what he had found. But he left some men behind to start a colony for Spain. A colony is a settlement that is ruled by another country.

Other Spaniards followed Columbus to the Americas. Some began Spanish colonies on islands in the Caribbean Sea. Others built colonies in North and South America.

One of the largest Spanish colonies was in Mexico. From Mexico, settlers moved north into the American Southwest. They built towns, churches, and forts in Florida, Texas, New Mexico, Arizona, and California. Today, Mexico and all the countries to its south are called Latin America.

People living in the United States whose ancestors were Spanish settlers are called **Latinos**. Some Latino families have lived here for many years. Others have just arrived. The largest group of Latinos came from Mexico. Others have come from Cuba, Puerto Rico, and the rest of Latin America.

Latinos people living in the United States whose ancestors were Spanish settlers

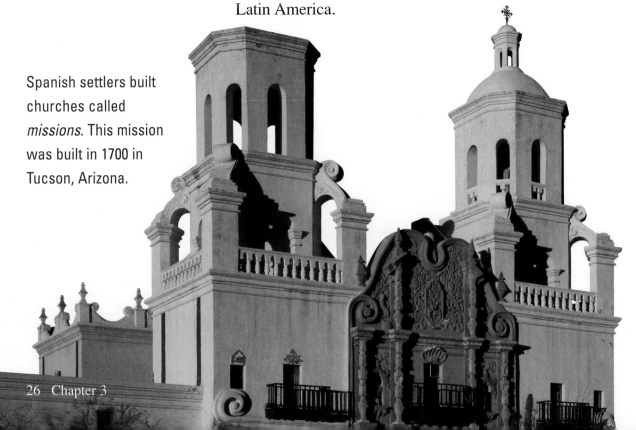

Spanish settlers built churches called *missions*. This mission was built in 1700 in Tucson, Arizona.

3.5 The Contributions of Latinos

Latinos have made many contributions to American life. One was their skill at mining. They taught people in the West how to mine gold, silver, and copper.

Another contribution was their skill at desert farming. Latinos showed Americans how to turn the dry Southwest into a rich farming region. Many crops grown in this region today were brought here from Mexico. These crops include oranges, grapes, and olives.

You have seen another contribution on television: the cowboy. Everything about cowboys came to America from Mexico—even the cows. Mexican settlers brought cattle to the Southwest. They brought the cattle ranch. And they brought the Mexican cowboy, called a *vaquero*.

Mexican *vaqueros,* or cowboys, wear large-brimmed hats to protect them from the sun all day.

Americans learned how to be cowboys from Mexican vaqueros. Their wide-brimmed cowboy hats came from Mexican *sombreros*. Their high-heeled cowboy boots came from Mexican *botas*. Mexican vaqueros taught Americans how to rope cattle using *la riata,* or the lariat. The vaqueros even taught the first singing cowboys how to play the Spanish guitar.

Here are still more Latino contributions to American life:

- *Holidays:* Cinco de Mayo, The Day of the Dead
- *Foods:* tacos, chili, burritos, corn chips, nachos, enchiladas, tamales, salsa, tortillas
- *Words:* barbecue, tornado, canyon, patio, hurricane, ranch, coyote, mosquito
- *Cool stuff:* ponchos, western saddles, guitars, Spanish-style buildings, lassos
- *Other gifts:* rodeos, Latino music and dancing, Spanish folk songs

This painting is called *The First Thanksgiving.*

3.6 More Europeans Come to America

The Spanish were the first Europeans to come to North America. But others soon followed. The French started a colony in Canada. Russians began a colony in Alaska. Dutch settlers built a colony in what is now New York.

Settlers from England began colonies on the eastern shore of North America. Between 1607 and 1733, the English built 13 colonies in America. These colonies hugged the Atlantic Coast from Maine to Georgia.

The 13 American colonies attracted settlers from many parts of Europe. Most were poor people. They came to find land or work. Others were searching for freedom to follow their religion. Still others came to escape jail. All hoped to start new lives in a new land.

In 1776, the American colonies broke away from England. Together they formed a new nation called the United States of America.

The new nation welcomed immigrants from Europe. An **immigrant** is a person who comes to live in a country from some other place. **European Americans** are the descendants of immigrants from Europe. A descendant is a person who comes from a certain group.

At first, most immigrants came from northern Europe. Later they came from eastern and southern Europe, as well. Each group added to America's diversity, or mix of peoples.

immigrant a person who comes to live in a country from another place
European Americans the descendants of immigrants from Europe

3.7 The Contributions of European Americans

European Americans played a large part in shaping American life. One great contribution was the English language. Americans speak English today because so many English colonists settled in the American colonies.

Many European Americans also liked to invent things. They invented new machines such as the telephone, radio, and electric lights. These inventions made life easier for people.

The American government is another contribution of European Americans. The United States is the world's oldest democracy. A democracy is a government ruled by the people.

The colonists from Europe soon became tired of being told what to do by a king. They wanted to govern, or rule, themselves. The king of England did not want to give Americans this freedom. He sent troops to America to keep the colonies under his control.

The colonists had to fight for their freedom. That fight is known as the American Revolution. They knew that freedom was worth fighting for.

The U.S. Capitol was built to look like buildings in the cities of Greece and Rome.

Here are still more European American contributions to American life:

- *Holidays:* Independence Day, Christmas, Hanukkah, Halloween
- *Foods:* cookies, hot dogs, hamburgers, pretzels, spaghetti, pizza, waffles, bagels
- *Words:* espresso, poodle, kindergarten, dock, dollar, denim, garage
- *Cool stuff:* skis, trains, violins, umbrellas, cars, bikes, radios, pianos, telephones
- *Other gifts:* ballet, opera, plays, classical music, poetry, paintings, bluegrass music

3.8 Africans Arrive in America

In 1619, a Dutch trading ship arrived in the colony of Virginia. The ship's captain made a deal with the colonists. He traded them 20 Africans for food.

These Africans did not come to the colonies of their own free will. They had been taken from Africa by force. Once in Virginia, they were sold as slaves. A slave is a person who is owned by another person.

Today we know that slavery is very wrong. But in 1619, the practice of buying and selling people was common in much of the world. In Africa, for example, people captured in wars were sold as slaves.

For almost 200 years, Africans were brought to this country against their will. Most were sold as slaves. They worked on farms raising tobacco, rice, and cotton. For this work, slaves received no pay. Many **African Americans** are the descendants of those unpaid workers.

Slavery became part of life in the American South. But outside the South, many people opposed slavery. The fight over slavery finally led to war in 1861. This war is known as the Civil War.

When the Civil War ended in 1865, slavery was dead. But African Americans' struggle to be treated like other Americans was just beginning.

This slave family picked cotton near Savannah, Georgia, in the late 1800s.

African Americans
descendants of people from Africa

3.9 The Contributions of African Americans

African Americans made many contributions to American life. In Africa, telling stories is an honored art. African Americans brought that art to America. We enjoy it today in books, plays, poetry, and rap music.

African Americans also helped create many styles of American music. These musical styles include gospel, jazz, rock and roll, and blues.

Perhaps their greatest contribution has been African Americans' fight for equal rights. Rights are freedoms that belong to all people.

The Civil War ended slavery in 1865. But it did not end prejudice against African Americans. Prejudice is an unfair opinion about people based on their skin color, background, or religion. Because of their dark skin, African Americans were often denied the same rights as white people.

African Americans fought long and hard for equal rights. Some people died in that struggle. Others went to jail. Laws were finally passed to end this unfair treatment.

Today all Americans—no matter what their skin color—are equal under the law. We all have equal rights because African Americans refused to accept anything less.

Here are still more African American contributions to American life:

- *Holidays:* Martin Luther King Day, Kwanza, Juneteenth
- *Foods:* soul food, corn bread, black-eyed peas, collard greens, gumbo, yams
- *Words:* banana, jazz, voodoo, jitterbug, jukebox, gorilla, tote, goober
- *Cool stuff:* banjos, drums, proverbs, quilts, 300 uses for peanuts, cosmetics
- *Other gifts:* ragtime music, spirituals, folktales, African American dance styles

Martin Luther King Jr. led the civil rights movement in the 1960s.

3.10 Asians Come to America

In 1848, gold was discovered in California. News of this discovery brought the first Chinese immigrants to the United States. Not all Americans welcomed the Chinese gold seekers. But they did admire how hard the Chinese worked.

As Americans moved west in the late 1800s, they had big dreams. They wanted to cross the country with railroad. They wanted to build new farms and factories. To make these dreams come true, they needed workers. The word went out across Asia: send workers!

Many Asian Americans helped build our railroad system. This train trestle, or bridge, is in the Sierra Nevada Mountains.

The Chinese came first. Between 1850 and 1930, about 400,000 Chinese came to America. Some saved their money and returned to China. But about half stayed in the United States.

Immigrants from Japan, Korea, and the Philippine Islands came next. Some went to Hawaii to work in the sugar fields. Others worked on farms and factories on the West Coast. One Japanese immigrant wrote this poem about going to America:

> *Huge dreams of fortune*
> *Go with me to foreign lands*
> *Across the ocean.*

Instead of fortune, most Asian immigrants found hard lives. They worked long hours for little pay. They were often treated roughly by their bosses. Still, most of them stayed in their adopted land. Today we call their descendants **Asian Americans**.

Asian Americans
descendants of Asian immigrants

3.11 The Contributions of Asian Americans

Asian Americans form one of the most diverse groups in the United States. Today, this group includes people from China, Japan, the Philippines, Korea, Vietnam, Cambodia, Laos, Thailand, India, and Pacific Island countries.

Asian Americans have made many contributions to American life. One is their way of preparing food. Asian immigrants brought new foods to the United States. They also brought new ways of cooking. As a result, Americans enjoy many kinds of Asian food today.

Another contribution is Asian Americans' respect for learning. Education has great value in Asian cultures. Asian Americans have continued that tradition.

Here are more Asian American contributions to American life:

- *Holidays:* Chinese New Year, Tet, Moon Festival
- *Foods:* chow mein, ketchup, sushi, ramen, kimchee, curry, tofu, potstickers
- *Words:* jungle, shampoo, kimono, bamboo, rattan, gingham, samurai, lei, tattoo
- *Cool stuff:* chopsticks, woks, hot tubs, acupuncture, rice cookers, surfboards
- *Other gifts:* origami, Japanese gardens, martial arts, yoga, luaus

To the Asian American culture, learning and education are very important.

3.12 Chapter Summary

Sooner or later, you will hear someone describe the United States as a nation of immigrants. It's true. All of us came to this land from some other place. Some made the journey thousands of years ago. Others arrived just yesterday.

Each group came for its own reasons. Native Americans followed the animals they hunted to a new land. The Spanish were looking for a route to Asia. The English came seeking freedom and opportunity. Other Europeans were fleeing war and hunger. Asians crossed the ocean to find gold and work. Africans were brought to America against their will.

Immigrants are still traveling to America. Most of these new immigrants come from Latin America and Asia. But people also come from other parts of the world.

In the next few chapters, you will meet people from the different groups that peopled our nation. And you will learn more about their contributions to American life.

These three girls have something in common. They are all Americans.

A Train Tour of the Northeast

4.1 Introduction

Welcome to our train tour of the historic Northeast. My name is Ms. Mariner. I will be your guide for the next few days. When not leading tours, I work in my town's local history center. So you'll hear a lot from me about the past as we go.

Our tour will take you to many different places. Each one has a story to tell about the Northeast and its people. As we visit these places, I want you to look for answers to three questions. First, why do we call the Northeast the "birthplace of our nation"? Next, why did our nation's first factories start here? And finally, what large cities are found in the Northeast? You'll hear and see clues to the answers to these questions as we travel along.

Watch your step as you climb aboard. Our first stop will be in the beautiful state of Maine.

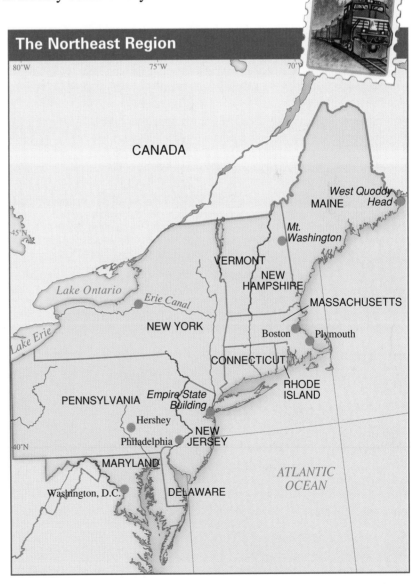

The Northeast Region

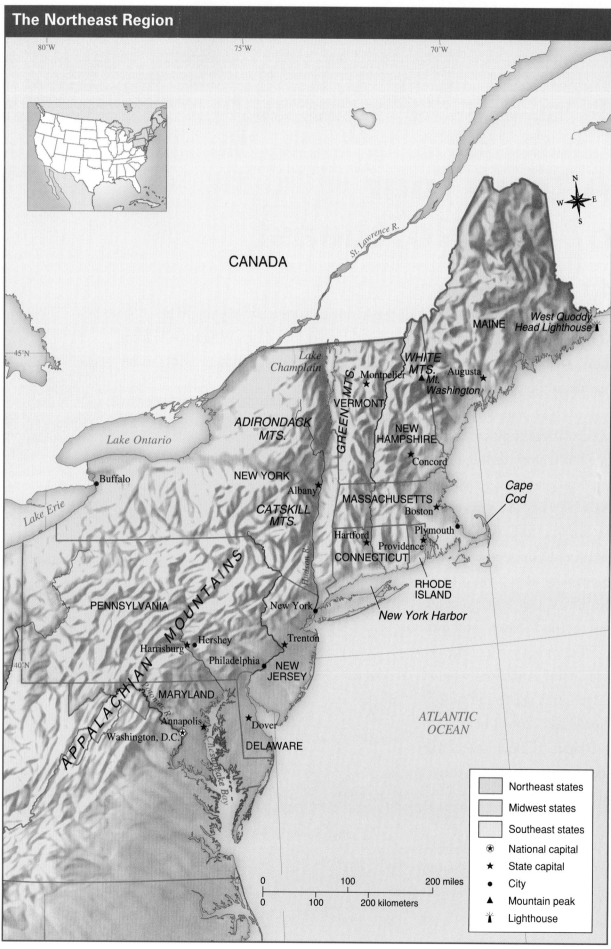

80°W   75°W   70°W

CANADA

St. Lawrence R.

45°N

MAINE

West Quoddy
Head Lighthouse

Lake
Champlain

WHITE
MTS.

Montpelier

Mt.
Washington

Augusta

VERMONT

GREEN MTS.

ADIRONDACK
MTS.

NEW
HAMPSHIRE

Lake Ontario

Concord

NEW YORK

Cape
Cod

Albany

MASSACHUSETTS

Buffalo

CATSKILL
MTS.

Boston

Lake Erie

Hartford

Plymouth

Providence

CONNECTICUT

Hudson R.

RHODE
ISLAND

New York

New York Harbor

PENNSYLVANIA

Trenton

APPALACHIAN MOUNTAINS

Hershey

Harrisburg

Philadelphia

NEW
JERSEY

MARYLAND

ATLANTIC
OCEAN

Potomac R.

Annapolis

Dover

Washington, D.C.

Chesapeake Bay

DELAWARE

	Northeast states
	Midwest states
	Southeast states
⊛	National capital
★	State capital
●	City
▲	Mountain peak
⚘	Lighthouse

0   100   200 miles
0   100   200 kilometers

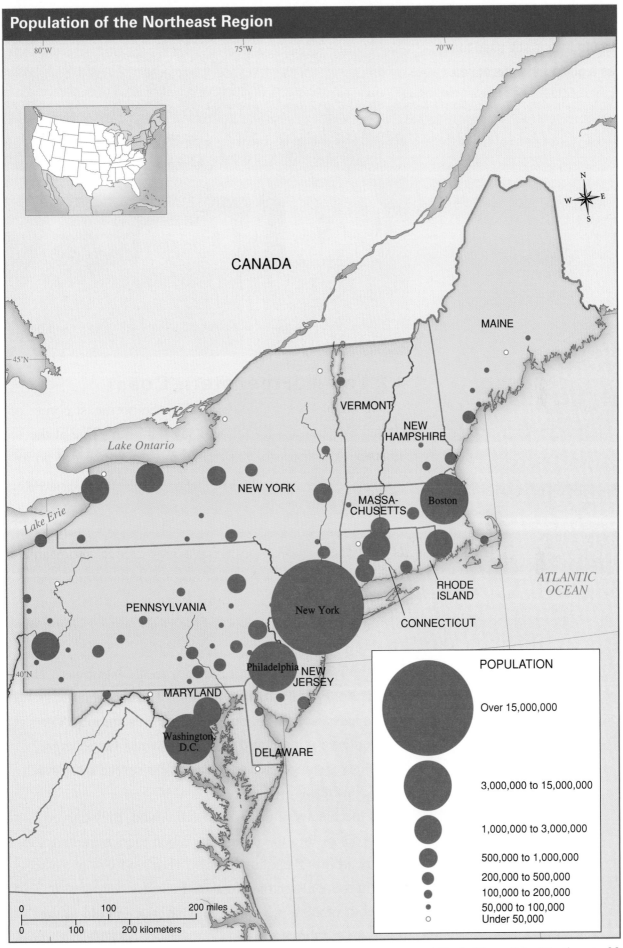

80°W   75°W   70°W

CANADA

MAINE

VERMONT

NEW
HAMPSHIRE

45°N

Lake Ontario

NEW YORK

MASSA-
CHUSETTS

Boston

Lake Erie

RHODE
ISLAND

ATLANTIC
OCEAN

PENNSYLVANIA

New York

CONNECTICUT

Philadelphia NEW
JERSEY

40°N

MARYLAND

Washington,
D.C.

DELAWARE

POPULATION

Over 15,000,000

3,000,000 to 15,000,000

1,000,000 to 3,000,000

500,000 to 1,000,000

200,000 to 500,000

100,000 to 200,000

50,000 to 100,000
Under 50,000

0   100   200 miles

0   100   200 kilometers

The West Quoddy Head Lighthouse is still used today as a guide for ships at sea.

4.2 The Northeastern Coast

We are at West Quoddy Head in the northeast corner of Maine. The Indians living here say that they "live at the sunrise." And they do. This is the most northeastern point of the United States. The sun rises here before anywhere else in the country.

The West Quoddy Head Lighthouse was built in 1858. Its light and foghorn keep ships from crashing into Maine's rocky shore. Some people find foghorns annoying—but not my grandfather. He trapped lobsters near here. "On a foggy day," he liked to say, "there is no prettier sound than a foghorn's moan."

Fishing is an important industry in the Northeast. The coast is dotted with fishing harbors. These harbors weren't always here. Long ago, this coastline was smooth. Then Earth entered a long cold period known as the *ice age.* Mile-thick sheets of ice called *glaciers* spread over much of the Northeast.

As the glaciers moved across the land, they carved deep grooves into the coastline. When the ice melted, the sea flowed into these low places. That's why you see so many harbors along the Northeast coast.

At our next stop, you'll see what glaciers did to the mountains of the Northeast.

4.3 The Mountains of the Northeast

Welcome to Mt. Washington in the state of New Hampshire. At 6,288 feet tall, Mt. Washington is the highest **peak** in the Northeast. On a clear day, visitors can see for a hundred miles.

Mt. Washington has some of the world's most severe weather. It can snow here all year long. The peak is also one of the windiest places on Earth.

My family visited Mt. Washington when I was your age. We rode the Mount Washington Cog Railway to the top. This mountain-climbing train runs on the second-steepest railway in the world. The wind speed that day was 75 miles per hour. My mother still believes that if she hadn't held on to me, I would have blown out to sea. The highest wind speed ever recorded here was 231 miles per hour. That was in 1934.

Mt. Washington is in the White Mountains of New Hampshire. The White Mountains are part of the Appalachian Mountain Range. The Appalachians are one of the oldest mountain ranges in the world.

peak the top of a mountain

Many hikers climb Mt. Washington each year.

4.4 Democracy Takes Root at Plymouth

This is Plymouth, Massachusetts. The Pilgrims landed here almost 400 years ago. You can see a reproduction of their ship, the *Mayflower,* in Plymouth Harbor.

In 1620, the *Mayflower* left England with 101 passengers. Half were Pilgrims going to America in search of religious freedom. Half were settlers bound for Virginia. The Pilgrims called these settlers "strangers."

Storms blew the *Mayflower* off course. Instead of Virginia, the ship reached New England. Sick of stormy seas, the Pilgrims decided to stop there. But they had a problem. There was no government in New England. And some of the strangers looked like trouble-

Visitors to Plymouth can step aboard the *Mayflower II,* a reproduction of the Pilgrims' ship.

makers. What would you have done in their situation? Think about this as you leave the train to visit Plymouth.

Welcome back. I'll tell you now how the Pilgrims solved their problem. Before going ashore, they drew up an agreement called the Mayflower Compact. It said they would set up a government and make laws for the good of everyone. Each man signed the compact. Then the passengers elected a governor.

democracy a form of government in which people vote for their laws and leaders

Today Americans believe that people should make their own laws and elect their own leaders. We call this form of government a **democracy**. During a time when kings and queens were in charge, this was a bold idea.

4.5 Boston Leads the Fight for Freedom

We are now at the Boston Common in Boston, Massachusetts. The Boston Common is America's first public park. Boston is one of America's oldest cities. It is also where the fight for America's freedom began.

In 1775, the people of the 13 colonies did not want to live under British rule anymore. Fighting broke out between colonists and British troops near Boston. This was the beginning of a long war called the American Revolution. The **revolution** led to the overthrow, or destruction, of British rule.

revolution the overthrow of a system of government

Two historic trails begin at the Boston Common. The first is the Freedom Trail. This walking tour takes you to places where the fight for freedom began. The trail ends at Bunker Hill. The first battle of the American Revolution was fought on this hill.

The second trail is the Black Heritage Trail. On this walking tour, you will learn about the long history of African Americans in Boston. The trail ends at the African Meeting House. This meeting house is the oldest African American church building in the United States.

Which trail should you take? I recommend both. Just be sure to wear good walking shoes.

The Old State House in Boston is one of the sights along the Freedom Trail.

4.6 The Erie Canal Links the Northeast and Midwest

Have you ever sung a song called "The Erie Canal"? You are looking at the canal that inspired the song. A **canal** is a ditch dug across land. It connects one waterway with another. The Erie Canal is a 363-mile-long ditch that connects the Hudson River with the Great Lakes.

Work on the Erie Canal began in 1817. At that time, there was no good way to move goods from the Northeast to the Midwest. Moving goods by horse and wagon was slow and costly. Moving goods by boat was faster and cheaper. But there was a problem. The Appalachian Mountains lay between the Midwest and the Northeast. No river crossed the mountains.

The men who built the Erie Canal solved that problem. They dug a 40-foot-wide ditch from the Hudson River to Lake Erie. Along the way, they built 83 locks to help carry boats over the mountains. **Locks** are used to raise and lower boats in the water.

The Erie Canal opened in 1825. It was an instant success. Freight prices between Lake Erie and New York City dropped from $100 a ton to just $10 a ton. New York City was soon the nation's busiest seaport.

This is just one small section of the Erie Canal. Can you see the lock in this photograph?

4.7 Hershey, Pennsylvania: A Town Built on Chocolate

One of my favorite movies is *Willy Wonka and the Chocolate Factory*. So, I was very excited when my family visited Hershey, Pennsylvania. At last I got a chance to see a real chocolate factory. Yum!

Later, I wondered why America's first factories were built in the Northeast. I think there are two main reasons. One reason is waterpower. The first factories were built alongside rivers. The rivers rushed down out of the mountains. This rushing water turned big waterwheels that made the machines in the factories run.

A second reason is people power. The Northeast was a good place for people who wanted to start businesses. Candy maker Milton Hershey was one of these people.

A hundred years ago, Milton Hershey started a candy business here in Pennsylvania. He used a system called mass production in his factory. **Mass production** is a way of making large quantities of the same product. The Hershey bar was America's first mass-produced candy bar. Today, Hershey's factory is the largest chocolate factory in the world.

We'll stop here to learn more about mass production. Enjoy your visit. And try not to eat too much chocolate.

At the chocolate factory in Hershey, Pennsylvania, streetlights are shaped like chocolate kisses. You can watch real chocolate kisses being made there.

mass production a way of making large quantities of the same product

4.8 Independence Hall: The Birthplace of the United States

You are looking at Independence Hall in Philadelphia, Pennsylvania. It was here that the United States was born. We celebrate our nation's birthday each year on Independence Day.

The first Independence Day was July 4, 1776. On that day, leaders from the 13 colonies met in Independence Hall to sign the Declaration of Independence. This statement told the world that Americans had formed their own nation. They called it the United States of America.

Americans fought a long war to win their independence. Great Britain finally agreed that Americans should govern themselves. But how would they do that?

In 1787, the nation's best thinkers met in Independence Hall to answer that question. They talked and argued for months. Then they wrote a new constitution, or plan of government, for the country. We still live under that plan today.

The **Constitution** is based on the idea of democracy. Under this plan, we, the people, choose our leaders. The Constitution also protects our rights. You have the right to say what you think. You may follow any religion. You have the right to a fair trial. These are rights that the Constitution, and all Americans, hold dear.

Today, Independence Hall is part of Independence National Historic Park in Philadelphia.

Constitution the plan of government for the United States

4.9 Washington, D.C.: Our Nation's Capital

Have you ever said to yourself, "There ought to be a law against this"? Well, you've come to the right place. You are looking at the United States Capitol. Our nation's laws are made right here.

Welcome to Washington, D.C. Washington is the capital of the United States. Our country's government is located here. The main business of this city is government.

The national government has three branches, or parts. Each has a different role.

The legislative branch makes laws for our country. This lawmaking branch is called Congress. Voters in each state elect lawmakers to represent them in Congress.

The president of the United States is head of the executive branch. The president's main job is to make sure that laws passed by Congress are carried out. Voters in all 50 states elect the president.

The judicial branch is made up of the courts. This branch guarantees that the laws passed by Congress are obeyed. The Supreme Court is the nation's highest court. One of its jobs is to make sure that laws passed by Congress follow the Constitution.

The Capitol Building in Washington, D.C., is where Congress meets to make our nation's laws.

The Empire State Building is 1,472 feet tall to the top of its antenna.

4.10 New York City: Where Buildings Touch the Sky

We are in New York City, the last stop on our tour of the Northeast. More than 8 million people live in New York City. It is the largest city in America.

New York has always been a city of immigrants. The Dutch were the first to settle here. People from other parts of Europe and Africa followed. Together they made New York City a city of many cultures, or groups of people.

Today people still come to New York City from all over the world. Just listen to people talking on the streets. You will hear English, Spanish, Chinese, Arabic, Russian, Hebrew, Italian, Korean, and many other languages.

Are you wondering how New York finds room for all these people? The answer is up in the air. A hundred years ago, New Yorkers began building **skyscrapers**. People live and work in these very tall buildings.

The Empire State Building is New York's most famous skyscraper. This office building has 102 stories, or floors. Visitors can go to the very top of the building and look out at the view. You could climb the 1,860 stairs. But I suggest you take the elevator.

skyscraper a very tall building

4.11 Chapter Summary

Do you remember the questions I asked you when we began our journey?

The first was why we call the Northeast the "birthplace of our nation." After visiting Boston and Philadelphia, you should know the answer. Boston is where the American Revolution began. And Philadelphia is where Americans first declared their independence from Great Britain.

I also asked you why the first factories were located in the Northeast. We talked about two reasons. The Northeast had a lot of waterpower for running factories. And it had people who enjoyed the challenge of starting new businesses.

Also, new methods of transportation encouraged people to build factories here. Canals and railroads lowered the cost of moving goods to customers.

My last question was which large cities are found here. You visited the four largest cities in the Northeast: Boston, Philadelphia, Washington, D.C., and New York City. You also stopped at two smaller towns, Plymouth and Hershey. Which city or town would you most like to visit again?

Our tour of the Northeast is ending now. I hope you enjoyed your trip as much as I enjoyed being your guide.

Vermont bursts into a blaze of color in autumn.

Population Density and Life in the Northeast

5.1 Introduction

This photograph shows the United States at night. Some areas look like bright dots of lights. Other areas are darker. The bright areas are where lots of people live. These are densely populated areas. People live close together in towns and cities there.

The dark areas are where fewer people live. These are sparsely populated areas. People live far apart there.

Look at the Northeast region in the photograph. Do you see the long, brightly lit area? This is the Northeast megalopolis. The word **megalopolis** means "great city."

This megalopolis is a string of densely populated towns and cities. It stretches 500 miles from Boston to Washington, D.C. We call this megalopolis "Boswash." In this chapter, you will read about how population density affects daily life in the Northeast.

Cities and Small Towns

5.2 Living in the Northeast

Where do you live? In a big city? In a medium-sized suburb? In a small town? In a rural area? Each of these places has a different **population density,** or number of people who live there. And that difference affects how the people live.

Population density is a measure of how many people live in a given amount of area. It is often shown as the number of people per square mile of land. The word *per* means "for each." A square mile is a square piece of land measuring one mile on each side.

Rural areas have fewer than 50 people per square mile. This means that there are fewer than 50 people living on each square mile of land. Urban areas have more than 500 people per square mile.

There are good things about living in both rural and urban areas. In small towns, people get to know each other. Folks often look out for their neighbors. Life is often quiet and peaceful there.

Cities may not seem as friendly as small towns. But they offer people more choices. There are many places to shop. Restaurants serve food from all over the world. And there is always something exciting to do in a city.

New York City has a population density of more than 23,000 people per square mile. Small towns in the Northeast are much less crowded.

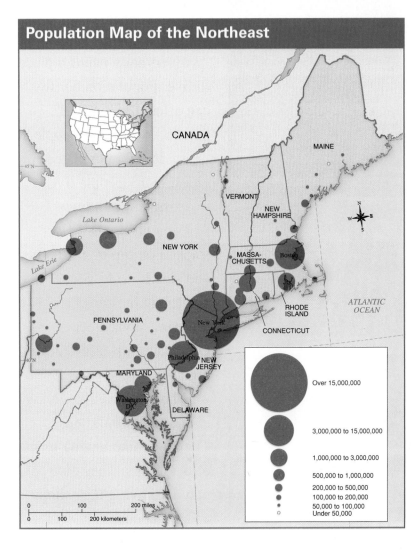

Population Map of the Northeast

5.3 Reading a Population Map

Maps can show many things about a place. The map on this page is a population map. A **population map** shows where people live in a region. It also shows how many people live in each area.

Look at the map key. Each circle stands for a different number of people. Which size circle shows the least populated, or rural, areas? Which size shows the most populated, or urban, areas?

Can you find the megalopolis Boswash on the map? It stretches from Massachusetts south through parts of Rhode Island, Connecticut, New York, New Jersey, Pennsylvania, Delaware, and Maryland. What do you notice about the population density of this area?

Now look at the states of Vermont, New Hampshire, and Maine on the map. How is the population density of these states different from that of Boswash?

population map a map showing where people live in a region or an area

Thousands of people may live on one city block. Just one small family may live on several acres in the country.

5.4 Places to Live

Everybody needs a place to live. Population density can affect the kinds of homes available to people.

In densely populated cities, many people live in apartment buildings. Apartments are usually stacked on top of each other and side by side. Some apartment buildings are towering skyscrapers. Others are just a few stories high.

Many people like living in apartment buildings. They may like having lots of neighbors. They also may like living near shops and restaurants.

On the other hand, neighbors can sometimes be noisy. People live close to each other in apartment buildings. People can't play loud music or make a lot of noise in an apartment. Well, they can—but their neighbors may not like it!

In small towns and rural areas, most people live in houses. A house usually has more space than an apartment. Houses have yards where children can play. People can make lots of noise in a house without bothering their neighbors.

However, taking care of a house and yard is a lot of work. Houses have to be painted. Lawns have to be mowed. And snow has to be shoveled in winter.

5.5 Making a Living

Population density also affects the kind of work people do. There are many more jobs in cities than in rural areas.

Small towns and rural areas have few businesses. Some people may work on a farm. Others may work in stores or provide services that people need. There are usually only a few kinds of jobs in a small town. That is one reason why people move to cities.

There are lots of different kinds of jobs in cities. Many people work in offices. Others work in restaurants, stores, and hotels.

Cities are communication centers. Newspapers, television stations, and book publishers have offices in cities. They create jobs for writers, photographers, and designers.

Cities also are centers for the arts. They attract people who want to work as actors, musicians, or artists.

Large hospitals and health care centers are located in cities. They create jobs for doctors, nurses, and many other health care workers.

Many people like to visit cities. Tourism is the business of taking care of tourists, or visitors. Tourism creates jobs for tour guides, hotel workers, taxicab drivers, and other workers.

A small town may have only one store. In a city, a new business may open every day.

5.6 Getting Around

Getting from place to place in a densely populated area can be difficult. Driving a car is usually the worst way to get around in big northeastern cities. Many of these cities' streets are narrow. Others are wide but crowded. Think of all the cars, buses, trucks, and taxis that fill city streets today. They cause traffic to move slowly.

It's not easy to find a place to park a car in a large city. Parking garages help solve this problem. But they can be expensive.

Bicycles fit well on narrow city streets. But riding a bike in city traffic can be dangerous.

Because city streets are often crowded, many people walk wherever they want to go in cities. For longer trips, people often use public buses, taxis, or subways.

In small towns and rural areas, it is hard to get around without a car. Driving is much easier in small towns than big cities. Traffic is not a problem.

Taxicabs may be a rare sight in a small town. Bicycles, however, are ridden everywhere.

Parking is usually free. And country roads are usually safe for both cars and bikes.

In less populated areas, many small towns have no public bus or taxi service. This can be a problem for people who don't drive or own a car.

5.7 People and Pollution

Population density also affects pollution. **Pollution** is anything that makes our air, water, or soil dirty or unsafe to use.

Many things we do cause pollution. When we toss trash on the ground, we pollute the land. When we drive cars, we pollute the air. When we dump waste into rivers, we pollute the water.

Pollution is a big problem in urban areas. People living in cities throw away mountains of trash each day. Some of the trash can be recycled. The rest must be carried off to dumps and landfills. If left on the streets, trash attracts insects and rats. These pests often carry harmful diseases.

Air pollution is a problem as well. Smoke from cars, factories, and homes can hover over cities. This dirty air can cause your eyes to burn. It can also damage your health.

Dirty water from city streets and sewers may run into rivers and lakes. The result is water pollution. Polluted water is not safe to drink or swim in.

In rural areas, there are fewer people to cause big pollution problems. Air and water are generally cleaner than in cities. At night, people can look up and see a million stars.

pollution any substance that makes air, water, or soil dirty or unsafe to use

Smog happens when fog mixes with smoke and other air pollution. Smog is not a problem in rural areas.

5.8 Finding Fun Things to Do

What do you do for fun on weekends? Your answer may depend partly on where you live.

People living in rural areas often enjoy outdoor activities. Many live close to good places to hike and fish in summer. In winter, they may go skiing or ice skating for fun. In winter or summer, they may go into town to see a movie or to meet friends at a restaurant.

In cities, people find many things to do close to home. On a sunny Saturday in New York City, you might
- go to a Yankees or Mets baseball game
- tour an aircraft carrier or an old sailing ship
- walk through a rain forest at the Bronx Zoo
- study bugs at the New York Botanical Garden
- ride the roller coaster at Coney Island

On a rainy Saturday in New York, you might
- climb the Statue of Liberty
- create a puppet at the Children's Museum of Art
- try indoor soccer or rock climbing at Chelsea Piers
- make a movie at the American Museum of the Moving Image
- see a circus or a play just for kids

People who live in the suburbs might choose to go to a city for a day of fun. And people who live in cities sometimes travel to the country for fun.

Sledding and skating are popular winter activities that are enjoyed in both the country and the city.

5.9 Chapter Summary

In this chapter, you learned how population density shapes people's daily lives. In the Northeast, many people live in densely populated areas. Others live in less populated areas. Life in a city is very different from life in a small town.

You saw how the number of people living in an area affects the kinds of homes people choose. People in cities often live in apartments. People in rural areas live in homes with yards.

You saw how population density affects the work people do. In rural areas, there are few jobs for fewer people. In cities, there are many more kinds of jobs.

You saw how population density affects transportation. People in cities often walk or use public transportation to get around. In rural areas, people depend on cars to get from place to place.

You saw how population density affects pollution. Cities often face serious pollution problems because of their large populations.

And you saw how population density affects what people do for fun. Suppose you could spend your next weekend anywhere in the Northeast. Where would you like to go? And what would you do for fun?

You can travel from a major city to a small farm in the Northeast in just a couple of hours.

MIAMI

GATOR XING
NEXT 1/2 MILE

NATCHEZ

chapter 6

A Boat and Bus Tour of the Southeast

6.1 Introduction

Hello. I'm Mr. Davis. You can probably tell from my uniform that I'm a park ranger. As part of my job, I get to take groups like yours on tours.

Usually I lead short walking tours. This trip is special. Over the next few days, we will tour the Southeast using three forms of transportation. Transportation is a way of moving people or goods. We will sail from Florida to Virginia on a fishing boat. From there we'll cross the Appalachian Mountains on a big bus. Then we'll board an old-time riverboat and sail down the Mississippi River.

As we travel, keep your eyes, ears, and minds wide open. Look at the land, and notice how it is used in different ways. Listen for sounds and music of this region. And think about how the Southeast has changed over time.

The captain says he's ready. So put on your life jackets, and let's go.

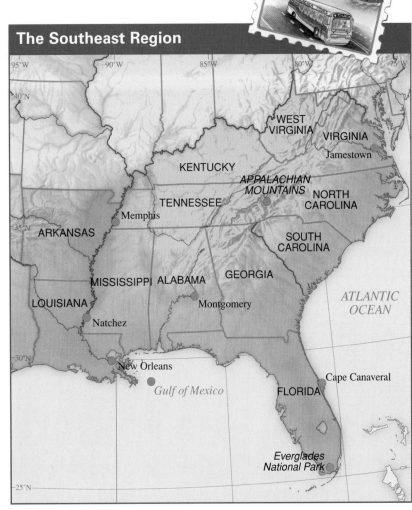

The Southeast Region

The Southeast Region

95°W · 90°W · 85°W · 80°W · 75°W

45°N

40°N

Ohio R.

WEST
VIRGINIA
★ Charleston

Shenandoah
National Park ■

Potomac R.

James R.

Richmond ★ ● Jamestown

VIRGINIA

★ Frankfort

KENTUCKY

APPALACHIAN MTS.

NORTH
CAROLINA ★ Raleigh

35°N

Nashville ★ TENNESSEE
*Great Smoky Mountains
National Park* ■

ARKANSAS

★ Little Rock

Hot Springs ■
National Park

SOUTH
Columbia ★
CAROLINA

ATLANTIC COASTAL PLAIN

● Atlanta

Mississippi R.

MISSISSIPPI   ALABAMA   GEORGIA

ATLANTIC
OCEAN

★ Jackson   Montgomery ★

Alabama R.

LOUISIANA

GULF COASTAL PLAIN

★ Tallahassee

30°N

Baton Rouge ★

FLORIDA

● Cape Canaveral

Gulf of Mexico

25°N

▨	Southeast states
▨	Midwest states
☐	Northeast states
▨	Southwest states
★	State capital
●	City
■	National Park
⚒	Oil drilling

0   100   200 miles

0   100   200 kilometers

Important Ports in the Southeast Region

95°W 90°W 85°W 80°W 75°W

45°N

40°N

WEST VIRGINIA

VIRGINIA

Hampton

Norfolk

KENTUCKY

NORTH CAROLINA

TENNESSEE

35°N

ARKANSAS

Wilmington

SOUTH CAROLINA

Charleston ATLANTIC OCEAN

MISSISSIPPI ALABAMA GEORGIA

Savannah

LOUISIANA

Jacksonville

Mobile

Baton Biloxi

Rouge Pensacola

Lake Pascagoula

Charles New

Orleans

30°N

FLORIDA

Tampa

Gulf of Mexico

Miami

25°N

⚓ Major port

0 100 200 miles

0 100 200 kilometers

Many waterways flow through the flat land of the Everglades.

6.2 Everglades National Park, Florida

You are looking at Everglades National Park in the state of Florida. A vast swamp covers the southern tip of Florida. It is known as the Everglades. A **swamp** is a low area of land that is covered by water at least part of the year.

My first job as a ranger was in Everglades National Park. I had studied geography in college and wanted to work in a real live swamp. But I had no idea just how alive it would be!

More than 300 kinds of birds live in the Everglades. I got up early one morning to record their calls on my pocket tape recorder.

What a racket! Alligators, crocodiles, turtles, snakes, and otters live in the park. So do deer, bear, panthers, bobcats, and rabbits.

The park looks peaceful now. But I was here in 1992 when Hurricane Andrew hit southern Florida. A **hurricane** is a dangerous storm with heavy rains and high winds. Andrew's winds destroyed the park visitor center. I recorded the sound of that storm at its worst. Whenever I listen to that tape, the roar of the winds gives me a chill.

swamp a low area of land that is covered by water at least part of the year

hurricane a storm with heavy rains and high winds

6.3 The John F. Kennedy Space Center at Cape Canaveral, Florida

Florida is in a part of the United States called the Sun Belt. The Sun Belt stretches across the country from Florida to California. States in the Sun Belt have a mild climate all year long. A mild climate means that it is usually warm and sunny there.

Florida's sunny climate makes it a popular place to visit. People from all over the world travel to Florida for vacations. People who travel for fun are called *tourists*.

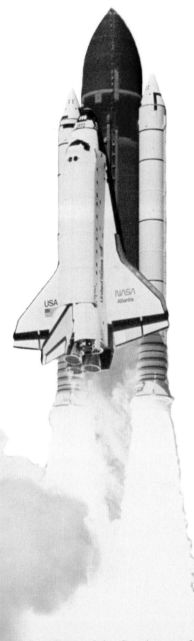

Rockets blast the space shuttle off its launch pad.

About 40 million tourists visit Florida every year. Some come to enjoy the sunshine and the beach. Others come to visit such places as Disney World and Cypress Gardens.

I like to visit the John F. Kennedy Space Center at Cape Canaveral. In 1961, Alan Shepard was launched into space from Cape Canaveral in a rocket. He was the first American in space. Today, Cape Canaveral is the home of the space shuttle.

Visitors to the Kennedy Space Center learn all about space exploration. They may even see a shuttle launch. I saw a launch last year and recorded the sound on my recorder. The rockets' blast was so loud that the ground shook under my feet.

6.4 Jamestown, Virginia: England's First American Colony

You are looking at the site of Jamestown, Virginia. Jamestown was the first permanent English settlement in America.

In the spring of 1607, settlers from England chose this spot on the James River to build a colony. John Smith, one of their leaders, called it "a very fit place." Wrong! The land was swampy. Mosquitoes made life miserable.

By summer, many people were sick. They were also hungry. The forests around Jamestown were full of food. But the colonists didn't know how to find it. By fall, more than half of them were dead. For many years, new colonists arrived each spring. By winter, most had died.

But, by 1619, things were looking up. The colonists found a crop that grew well around here. It was tobacco. Virginia tobacco sold well in England. The colony began to make money.

That same year, a Dutch ship arrived. Its cargo included 20 Africans. They were sold to the colonists as servants and slaves. This was the beginning of slavery in the colonies.

My ancestors were Africans. An **ancestor** is a relative who lived long ago. They were brought to America to be slaves. I often wonder whether any of my ancestors were on that Dutch ship.

ancestor a relative who lived long ago

Today, you can get a feel for 17th-century life at historic Jamestown settlement.

6.5 A Coal Mine in Appalachia

Welcome to Appalachia. This mountainous region is located in the southern part of the Appalachian Mountain Range. Appalachia has no exact borders. It covers most of West Virginia and parts of 12 other states, including North Carolina, South Carolina, and Georgia.

Appalachia is too hilly for much farming. But it is rich in minerals. **Minerals** are natural substances found in rocks. The region's most important mineral is coal. Coal is used to heat homes and produce electricity. About half of this country's electric power comes from burning coal.

In the past, miners dug tunnels into the Appalachian Mountains to get at the coal hidden inside. These underground mines were dangerous places. Many people died in mining accidents.

Today most coal comes from strip mines like the one you see here. **Strip mines** are surface mines. Miners use heavy machinery to strip away the dirt and rocks covering the coal. Then they use giant shovels to dig the coal out of the mountain.

Last fall I went to a bluegrass music festival near this mine. Bluegrass is the traditional music of Appalachia. It is played on banjos, guitars, and fiddles. I recorded a lot of old songs. The fast beat of this music always makes me feel good.

Coal is dug out of strip mines such as this one.

mineral a natural material found in rock
strip mine a place where minerals are scraped from the surface of the ground

Riverboats still cruise the Mississippi River.

6.6 Musical Memphis, Tennessee

We've reached Memphis, Tennessee. From now on, we'll be traveling in a riverboat like the one you see here.

Memphis is in the center of the Mississippi Delta region. The Mississippi Delta is a large area of land. It stretches from Kentucky and Arkansas to the mouth of the Mississippi River. A river's mouth is where it empties into the ocean.

A **delta** is a triangle-shaped area at the end of a river. Soil carried downstream by the river builds up to make a delta. Delta soil is fertile and good for farming.

In the early 1800s, that rich soil attracted cotton planters to this region. At that time, cotton was a valuable crop. Many planters brought slaves with them. Slaves did most of the work of planting and picking cotton.

Slaves led hard lives. They worked from sunup to sundown most days of the year. They had no right to choose what they wanted to do. They could be bought and sold like cattle.

Sometimes slaves would sing about their sorrows. These sad songs came to be known as the blues. In 1912, an African American songwriter in Memphis wrote the first popular blues song. He called it "Memphis Blues." Today Memphis is famous around the world as the home of the blues.

delta a triangle-shaped area of land at the end of a river

6.7 The French Quarter in New Orleans, Louisiana

Welcome to New Orleans, the largest city in Louisiana. French colonists built the city. It is near the mouth of the Mississippi River. You can see the homes of the colonists here in the French Quarter.

Ships from all over the world come to New Orleans. It is an important port in the United States. A port is place where ships load and unload their goods.

New Orleans is also the birthplace of **jazz**. African American musicians living near here created this new style of music. The best known is probably the great trumpet player Louis Armstrong. There are many kinds of jazz. One of the oldest is called Dixieland. You can hear great Dixieland jazz right here in the French Quarter.

Louisiana's nickname is the Bayou State. A **bayou** is a stream flowing through swampy land. In the 1700s, French colonists from Canada settled along Louisiana's bayous. They called themselves Acadians. Over time, the name was shortened to Cajuns.

Cajuns and their way of life used to be hidden away in the bayous. Not any more! Cajun food is all the rage in New Orleans. It's hot, spicy, and delicious. Cajun music is even more popular. It's as spicy as Cajun food—and it makes your toes tap!

jazz a kind of music
bayou a stream that flows through a swamp

The French Quarter is the oldest neighborhood in New Orleans. It is the part of the city that most tourists visit.

6.8 An Oil Rig in the Gulf of Mexico

Our riverboat is now in the Gulf of Mexico. We're heading out toward an oil rig. Many people who live near the Gulf Coast are oil workers. Another name for oil is **petroleum**. The state of Louisiana has 23,000 wells that pump petroleum, or oil, out of the ground.

Petroleum is a thick, black, oily liquid that is found deep in the earth and under the ocean floor. Drilling for oil under the ocean is not easy. Oil workers build huge platforms, called *rigs,* to hold their machinery. Then they drill down under the sea until they find oil.

Once the oil is pumped out of the earth, it is sent to a factory. This factory is called a *refinery.* It turns petroleum into useful products. The product you probably know best is gasoline for cars.

Oil is also used to make petrochemicals. That's a big word that means chemicals made from oil. Petrochemicals are used in all kinds of products, from medicines to plastics. I'll bet you're wearing a petrochemical product right now. It might be a button, a zipper, or the soles of your shoes.

Oil rigs like this one can be seen from shore all along the Gulf of Mexico.

6.9 A Cotton Plantation in Natchez, Mississippi

We are looking at a plantation home in Natchez, Mississippi. A **plantation** is a large farm.

In the early 1800s, cotton planters settled this area. Many of them grew very rich growing cotton. They spent their wealth building big homes like this one. Then they filled their homes with the best things money could buy.

All of this wealth depended on having slaves to work the land. President Abraham Lincoln believed slavery was wrong. So did many other people in the country. Southern planters did not agree.

It took a war to settle this argument. The American Civil War lasted four long years. Much of the Southeast was damaged in the fighting. More than 600,000 people died.

One good thing came out of this terrible war. Slavery was ended forever. I wonder how my slave ancestors felt when they heard they were free. It must have been an amazing feeling.

Natchez escaped the fighting. Its beautiful homes were not hurt in the war. Today they are the city's main tourist attraction.

plantation a large farm

Elaborate architecture was used for many plantation homes, such as this one in Natchez, Mississippi.

The Civil Rights Memorial displays the names of all the people who gave their lives in the civil rights movement.

6.10 Montgomery, Alabama: Birthplace of the Civil Rights Movement

You are looking at the Civil Rights Memorial in Montgomery, Alabama. This memorial honors 40 Americans who were killed during the civil rights movement.

After the Civil War, blacks in the South were free. But they were denied many of the rights other citizens had. At the same time, segregation became a way of life. **Segregation** is the separation of people because of race. African Americans could not go to school with whites. They could not eat at white lunch counters. They could not sit beside whites on a bus.

The civil rights movement began as a struggle to end segregation. It started here in Montgomery in 1955. That year a preacher named Martin Luther King Jr. led a protest against segregation on buses. African Americans in Montgomery refused to ride the buses until they were treated the same as whites.

Most African Americans back then did not have cars. My grandma walked to work every day for a year rather than ride a segregated bus. But finally, bus segregation was ended in Montgomery.

When I was little, I asked my grandma how her feet held up during the protest. "Child," she said, "my feet were tired, but my soul was rested."

segregation separation of people because of race

6.11 Chapter Summary

Do you remember what I said to you when we began our journey? I asked you to keep your eyes, ears, and minds wide open. Now I'll tell you why.

I wanted you to use your eyes to see different ways land is used in the Southeast. In Everglades National Park, for example, you saw land that people are working to preserve. But, in Appalachia, you saw a mountain that is being torn apart for the coal it contains.

You also saw four settlements built beside rivers. Three of them grew into cities. One did not. Can you figure out why?

I wanted you to use your ears to hear some of the sounds of the Southeast. As a park ranger, I enjoy the sounds of nature—even the roar of a hurricane. But most of all, I love the music of this region. From bluegrass to the blues, the Southeast has given this country a lot of great music.

Finally, I wanted you to learn how the Southeast has changed over time. Slavery and segregation are part of this region's past. But not its future. As my grandma likes to say, "Times have changed, child, and they've changed for the better."

Trees line the driveway at this plantation in North Carolina.

chapter 7

The Effects of Geography on Life in the Southeast

7.1 Introduction

What did you bring to school for lunch today? For some of you, the answer may be "a bit of the Southeast."

Start with the lunch bag itself. It may be made of paper that came from a southern pine tree. Papermaking is an important industry in the Southeast.

What's in the bag? A peanut butter and jelly sandwich? Orange juice? A piece of fruit? Much of a typical lunch could have come from the Southeast. Georgia grows more peanuts than any other state. Florida grows four out of five of our nation's oranges. Even the plastic wrap on the sandwich may have been made from oil found in the Southeast.

In this chapter, you will find out why so much of the Southeast is found in your lunch bags. At the same time, you will see how geography has shaped life in the Southeast today.

Geographic Features of the Southeast

A marsh is seen at low tide in Savannah, Georgia.

tidewater low-lying land along the coast

foothills a hilly region at the base of a mountain range

Fog rolls through Great Smoky Mountains National Park in North Carolina.

7.2 Elevation: Lowlands and Highlands

The Southeast is a region of lowlands and highlands. The low Coastal Plain stretches along the southeastern coast from Virginia to Louisiana. When the ocean rises each day at high tide, seawater flows into this lowland. The water level in rivers and swamps rises with the tide. As the tide drops, water levels drop. For this reason, Southerners call their coastal lowlands the **tidewater**.

The Coastal Plain ends at the **foothills** of the Appalachian Mountains. Southerners call this area of low, rolling hills the Piedmont. Piedmont means "foot of the mountains" in French. Beyond the Piedmont rise the highlands of the Appalachians. Some of the peaks are more than 6,000 feet high.

Elevation affects life here in many ways. For example, elevation affects climate. The higher the elevation of a place, the colder it is. Plants that grow well in the warm lowlands freeze in the cool highlands. It also affects soil. Lowland soil is rich and good for farming. Highland soil is rocky and not easy to farm.

Travel is also affected by elevation. Travel in the lowlands is fast and easy. Travel in the highlands is slow and difficult. Mountain people joke that the only way to get to some tiny Appalachian towns is to be born there!

7.3 Rivers and Ocean

The Southeast has a long coastline and many rivers. Most of its rivers begin in the Appalachian Mountains. On the eastern side of the Appalachians, rivers flow across the Piedmont and Coastal Plain to the Atlantic Ocean. In the southern Appalachians, rivers flow into the Gulf of Mexico. On the western side of the mountains, they flow into the Mississippi River.

Southerners use their ocean and rivers for recreation. Swimming, fishing, and boating are popular water sports.

People here also use the ocean and rivers for transportation. Shipping by boat is an inexpensive way to move crops and goods over long distances.

Many port cities have grown up along the coast where rivers reach the sea. One of the busiest port cities is Miami. Miami is located near the southern tip of Florida. Much of its trade is with countries in Central and South America. For this reason, Miami calls itself the "Gateway of the Americas."

The port of Miami is home to many cruise ships. Each year, more than 3 million people leave Miami on cruise ships for vacations at sea. No wonder Miami is also known as the "Cruise Capital of the World."

An oil tanker glides along the Mississippi River.

The Effects of Geography on Life in the Southeast   77

7.4 The Fall Line

Many of the rivers that cross the Coastal Plain are navigable. A **navigable** river is one that is wide and deep enough for ships to use. But when ships reach the Piedmont, they stop. The place where they stop is called the *fall line*.

The fall line is the line where the Piedmont meets the Coastal Plain. The edge of the Piedmont drops sharply at this point. As rivers flow over this drop, they form waterfalls. Ships cannot climb these falls to reach the Piedmont.

For early settlers in the Southeast, the fall line was a problem. Settlers on the Coastal Plain depended on rivers to send their crops to market. But when settlers moved up onto the Piedmont, they had no good way to ship their crops to the coast.

Some saw this problem as an opportunity. Traders set up trading posts right on the fall line. They traded goods that arrived by boat from the coast for meat and crops raised in the highlands.

Others settled on the fall line because they knew how to use falling water to run machines. They built sawmills, flour mills, and workshops that ran on waterpower.

Many fall-line towns—like Richmond, Virginia; Raleigh, North Carolina; and Macon, Georgia—grew into large cities.

navigable deep and wide enough for ships

This rocky section of the Potomac River flows near Washington, D.C.

7.5 Natural Resources

The Southeast is rich in natural resources. Natural resources include land, oceans, forests, minerals, and fuels.

Land was the first natural resource that attracted people to the Southeast. Growing crops and raising animals was the Southeast's largest industry for many years. An industry is all the businesses that produce one kind of good or provide one kind of service.

Today, many industries are important to the economy of the region. On your tour of the Southeast, you learned about two industries based on resources hidden under the ground. One is the coal-mining industry. Another is the oil industry.

The Southeast's steel industry is built on another hidden resource. In 1860, iron ore was found on Red Mountain in Alabama. Iron ore is used to make steel. Birmingham, Alabama, was built at the foot of Red Mountain as a steel-making center.

Some industries are based on the Southeast's large forests. Sawmills cut trees into lumber. Paper mills grind wood into gooey wood pulp. This pulp is then used to make paper. Furniture makers turn trees into tables and chairs. You may be sitting on a chair made in the Southeast.

Forested land is an important natural resource to the state of North Carolina.

The Effects of Geography on Life in the Southeast 79

This field of white, fluffy cotton is ready for picking.

agriculture the business of growing crops and raising animals

7.6 A Long Growing Season

Agriculture is an important part of the economy of the Southeast. **Agriculture** is the business of growing crops and raising animals. For farmers to succeed in this business, they need three things from nature. These things are good soil, plenty of rain, and a long growing season. The Southeast has all three.

Many crops grow well in the Southeast. Cotton is a good example. Cotton plants need six months of warm weather and plenty of water. The Southeast meets these needs perfectly.

In the 1800s, cotton was the main crop grown in the Southeast. Then disaster struck. A little bug called the *boll weevil* invaded cotton fields. The boll weevil destroyed the cotton before it was ready for harvest. Many farmers were ruined. Those who survived learned a hard lesson. No longer could they depend on just one crop.

Today the Southeast is a region of mixed agriculture. Farmers on the Coastal Plain grow rice, cotton, peanuts, and other warm-weather crops. Orange groves cover large parts of Florida. Piedmont farmers raise dairy cattle, peaches, and tobacco. Farmers in Appalachia grow corn and apples in mountain valleys.

Florida is a major grower of citrus fruit, including oranges, limes, grapefruit, and tangerines.

Damage from hurricanes is a result of high wind and floodwater.

floodplain low, flat land along a river that may be underwater during a flood

7.7 Dangerous Weather

Not every day is sunny in the Southeast. Rain falls all year long. Sometimes too much rain comes down. The result can be a flood.

Most rivers flood from time to time. During a flood, a river fills with more water than it can hold. The extra water flows over the river's banks, onto its floodplain. A **floodplain** is low, flat land along a river.

Floods become dangerous when people live and work on floodplains. Then floods do much more than cover the floodplain with muddy water. They destroy homes, crops, and people's lives.

The most dangerous storms are hurricanes. Hurricanes form over the Atlantic Ocean every summer. Almost every year, at lease one of them strikes the Southeast.

In 1992, a hurricane known as Andrew roared across southern Florida. Winds of up to 175 miles per hour smashed everything in the storm's path. About 250,000 people were left homeless.

From Florida, Andrew moved on to Louisiana. More than a million people fled inland as huge waves and high winds pounded the Louisiana coast.

When the storm ended, folks returned to clean up the damage and rebuild their homes. For Southerners, hurricanes, like floods, are a part of life.

7.8 Chapter Summary

Imagine that you could visit any town in the Southeast. Suppose you asked people how the geography of their area is important to their town. What do you think they would say?

If you were in Miami, Florida, people might talk about the importance of the ocean. Miami's beaches attract tourists to the city. Many jobs in Miami depend on the ocean.

In Dawson, Georgia, you might hear about the importance of a long growing season. Making peanut butter is a large industry in Dawson. People here know that peanuts need four to five months of warm weather to grow.

In New Iberia, Louisiana, people might talk about dangerous weather. Hurricane Andrew hit New Iberia with winds of more than 150 miles per hour.

In High Point, North Carolina, folks might mention the importance of forests. This town depends on wood from southeastern forests. Its main industry is making furniture. High Point produces so much furniture that it is called the "Furniture Capital of America."

In other towns, you would hear different answers. But no matter where you went, you would find that geography helps shape how people live in the Southeast.

The flat land and central location of Atlanta, Georgia, made it the perfect junction for railroads in the 1830s. Today it is one of the Southeast's largest cities.

A Crop Duster Tour of the Midwest

8.1 Introduction

Hi. My name is Mr. Ortiz. I'll be your guide as we explore the amazing Midwest. I'm an economist, and I work at a bank in Chicago. My boss gave me time off to lead your tour, for two reasons. The bank wants you to learn about the Midwest and its economy. Also, my boss knows I love to travel.

We will visit nine of my favorite places in the Midwest. Along the way, look for answers to this question: How did this one region earn these two very different nicknames: "America's Breadbasket" and "America's Heartland"?

We will be touring in little planes called *crop dusters*. Most of the time, these planes are used to spray crops with chemicals. Because of their small size, crop dusters can fly close to the ground. That means we'll get great views.

Fasten your seat belts for takeoff. Our first stop will be in the "show-me" state of Missouri.

The Midwest Region

CANADA
Lake Superior
Soo Locks
NORTH DAKOTA
MINNESOTA
Lake Huron
SOUTH DAKOTA
Mall of America
WISCONSIN
Lake Michigan
MICHIGAN
Mt. Rushmore
Detroit
Lake Erie
O'Hare Airport
Cedar Rapids
IOWA
Wrigley Field
NEBRASKA
OHIO
INDIANA
ILLINOIS
St. Louis
KANSAS
MISSOURI
Dodge City

The Midwest Region

100°W   95°W   90°W   85°W   80°W

50°N

Lake of the Woods

CANADA

Isle Royale National Park

Lake Superior

Soo Locks

NORTH DAKOTA

★ Bismarck

45°N

MINNESOTA

Lake Huron

SOUTH DAKOTA

St. Paul

★ Pierre

WISCONSIN

MICHIGAN

BLACK HILLS

Mall of America

Mississippi R.

Madison ★

Lansing

■ Mt. Rushmore Memorial

Lake Michigan

Detroit

Lake Erie

G R E A T

Missouri R.

IOWA

O'Hare Airport

Wrigley Field

Cleveland

NEBRASKA

Des Moines ★

Chicago

OHIO

Columbus ★

P L A I N S

★ Lincoln

40°N

ILLINOIS

INDIANA

Springfield ★

Indianapolis ★

MISSOURI

★ Topeka

Kansas City

Jefferson City ★

St. Louis

Ohio R.

KANSAS

35°N

Dodge City

N
W   E
S

30°N

Gulf of Mexico

MEXICO

25°N

0   100   200 miles
0   100   200 kilometers

★ State capital
● City
■ Point of interest

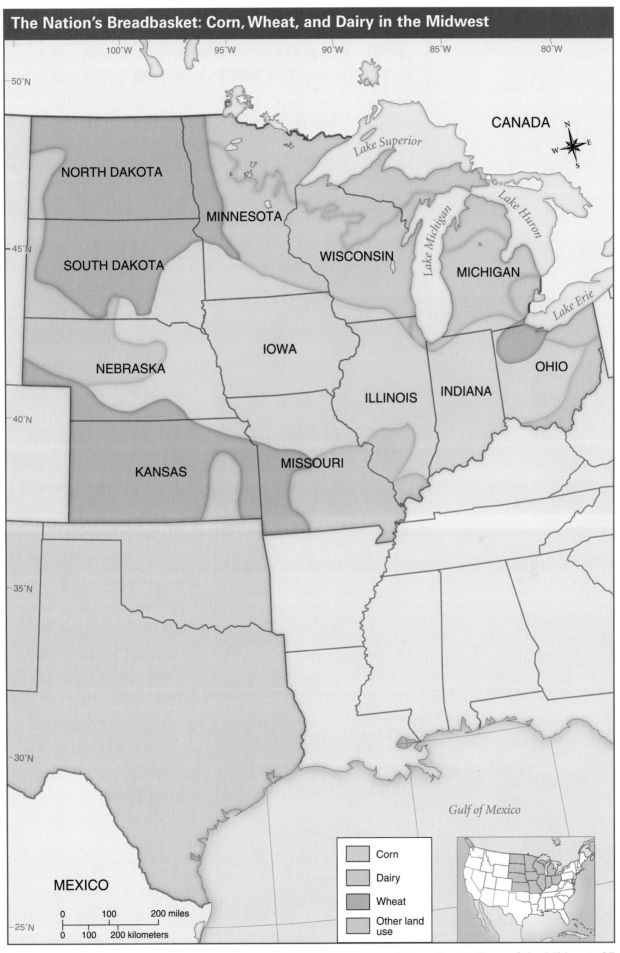

The Nation's Breadbasket: Corn, Wheat, and Dairy in the Midwest

CANADA

Lake Superior

Lake Michigan

Lake Huron

Lake Erie

NORTH DAKOTA

MINNESOTA

WISCONSIN

MICHIGAN

SOUTH DAKOTA

NEBRASKA

IOWA

ILLINOIS

INDIANA

OHIO

KANSAS

MISSOURI

MEXICO

Gulf of Mexico

Corn

Dairy

Wheat

Other land use

0   100   200 miles

0   100   200 kilometers

8.2 St. Louis, Missouri: Gateway to the West

Welcome to St. Louis, Missouri, and its Gateway Arch. I chose St. Louis as our first stop because of its history. This is where the settlement of the West and Midwest began.

St. Louis began as a frontier town. The **frontier** is where wild country begins. French traders first settled St. Louis. They chose this spot because it is near two mighty rivers. The Mississippi and Missouri Rivers come together just north of St. Louis.

frontier the beginning of unexplored land

Pioneers were the first people to settle the West. They started their journey by heading west from St. Louis. This is why St. Louis is called the "Gateway to the West." The Gateway Arch was built to honor those pioneers. It is a proud reminder of St. Louis's history.

The Gateway Arch is one of the most famous arches in the world. Made of gleaming stainless steel, it rises about 630 feet above the Mississippi River. Visitors can ride a tram to the top. I did this a few years ago with my family. My daughter said it was like riding in a big clothes dryer. The cars are small—but the view from the top is great.

The Gateway Arch in St. Louis is a memorial to the pioneers who first explored the West.

8.3 The Farm State of Iowa

If you wanted to invent a farming state, you couldn't do much better than Iowa. That's what my best friend from college said. He grew up on an Iowa farm that looks a lot like the one you see here.

"First," he said, "you'd want your farm state to be flat." Iowa began as flat prairie country. A **prairie** is an area of flat or rolling land covered mostly with tall grasses. Later, farmers planted crops on the flat prairie.

Next, you'd want **fertile** soil. Fertile means able to produce good crops. Iowa has so much fertile soil that farms cover almost every inch of the state.

Finally, you'd want good transportation. Iowa lies smack dab between the Mississippi and Missouri Rivers. Long before there were trains, Iowa farmers used these rivers to send their crops to market.

Today, Iowa farms produce huge crops of corn, soybeans, oats, and hay. Much of this harvest is fed to livestock. **Livestock** are animals raised on farms, such as cattle, hogs, and chickens. Iowa farm products are used in all kinds of foods. The chances are good that the next bag of popcorn you pop was grown on an Iowa farm just like this one.

From the air, the state of Iowa looks like one big farm.

prairie flat or gently rolling land that is covered with tall grasses and wildflowers

fertile soil able to produce good crops

livestock animals raised on farms, such as cattle

8.4 Dodge City, Kansas: Where the Cattle Still Roam

Welcome to Dodge City, Kansas. Kansas is famous for cowboys and wheat. Kansas produces more wheat than any other state. In areas too dry for wheat farming, cattle still roam the Kansas plains.

I was born in Dodge City. My parents came here from Mexico to work in a meatpacking plant. **Meatpacking** is the preparing of meat for sale. It's an important industry in the Midwest.

Back in the 1870s, cowboys from Texas used to drive cattle to Dodge City. These cattle drives took weeks or months. The cattle were loaded onto trains in Dodge City and shipped east for sale. The cowboys back then were a wild bunch. They made so much trouble that Dodge City was called "the wickedest little city in America."

When I was your age, I wanted to be a cowboy—or as my dad would say, a *vaquero*. Then I spent a summer on a ranch. Herding cattle, I discovered, is hot, dusty, smelly work. When cattle are upset, they can charge and knock you flat. But I have friends who are cowboys. Some just like working with animals. Others love working outdoors.

We'll stop here to learn more about cowboys. Watch out—some cowboys today ride motorcycles instead of horses.

meatpacking the preparing of meat for sale

When cowboys move large herds of cattle from one place to another, it's called a *cattle drive*.

8.5 South Dakota's Heroes

Two huge monuments are carved into the Black Hills of South Dakota. The first is Mt. Rushmore National Memorial. It shows the faces of four American presidents: George Washington, Thomas Jefferson, Theodore Roosevelt, and Abraham Lincoln. Each head is six stories tall.

The second monument honors a Sioux Indian chief named Crazy Horse. It is still being carved into the Black Hills. When it is finished, Crazy Horse Memorial will be the world's largest statue.

The Black Hills are sacred to the Sioux and other Native Americans. When settlers began moving into this area, Native Americans tried to keep them out. This struggle led to war with the United States.

During that war, an American soldier named George Custer attacked Sioux Indians camping by Little Big Horn River in Montana. Crazy Horse led his warriors into battle yelling, "It is a good day to die!" In minutes, Custer and his men were dead.

Despite this victory, the Sioux lost most of their land. Like other Native Americans, they were forced to live on **reservations,** or special areas set aside for their use.

My family and I visited both of these monuments last summer. My son summed up the trip in two words: "Totally awesome."

Mt. Rushmore National Memorial honors four American presidents.

reservation land set aside for Native Americans

This large monument honors Sioux chief Crazy Horse.

A Crop Duster Tour of the Midwest 91

The water in Lake Huron is lower than the water in Lake Superior. The Soo Locks allow boats like this tanker to travel between these two bodies of water.

8.6 Michigan's Soo Locks: Linking the Great Lakes

You are looking down on one of my favorite sights: the Soo Locks. The Soo Locks are the two longest locks in the world. They can lift and lower ships up to 1,000 feet long.

The Great Lakes are part of a water highway stretching from the Midwest to the Atlantic Ocean. Ships move from lake to lake along canals. However, the lakes are not all at the same level. Locks are needed to lift and lower ships from one lake to the next. The Soo Locks lift ships from Lake Huron up 21 feet to Lake Superior.

Many ships pass through the Soo Locks each day. Some are small passenger boats. Others are oceangoing ships filled with iron ore, coal, grain, or other cargo. Folks call them "salties" because they come from the Atlantic Ocean.

When I took my kids to Soo Locks, they thought the trip would be "boring." They didn't want another lesson from me about how important water transportation is to the economy of the Midwest. But then we got to the viewing area. A big salty was just entering the lock. We stood so close we could almost touch it. Now my kids can't wait to go back.

8.7 Detroit, Michigan: America's Motor City

In 1896, a Michigan farm boy named Henry Ford built his first car. At that time, automobiles were very expensive. People saw cars as toys for the rich.

But Ford had different ideas. He dreamed of building cars that most people could afford. Ford's dream gave birth to the American automobile industry.

In 1908, Ford started an automobile factory in Detroit, Michigan. He needed a way to keep his costs down. First he found a way to produce, all at once, the hundreds of parts that would go into his cars. This is the process called *mass production*. Still, it took many hours to assemble these parts into automobiles.

Ford solved that problem by installing a moving **assembly line**. A moving belt carried unfinished cars past workers. Each worker did one task. One might install a windshield. Another might screw on a door handle. The time needed to assemble a car dropped from 12 hours to just 93 minutes.

Ford's success brought other car makers to Detroit. Before long, Detroit was known as "Motor City," or "Motown" for short.

The automobile industry attracted other businesses to the Midwest. Today, industry is as important as farming in many Midwestern states.

assembly line a process in which each worker does one part of a job before passing it on to the next worker

These Model T's were built on Ford's assembly line in the early 1900s.

8.8 O'Hare International Airport: The Midwest's Transportation Hub

You are looking at O'Hare International Airport in Chicago, Illinois. Travelers voted O'Hare the "Best Airport in North America" in the year 2000. It is also one of our busiest airports. About 200,000 people pass through O'Hare each day. That adds up to about 73 million airplane passengers a year.

Chicago has always been a **transportation hub,** or a center for moving goods and people. In the 1800s, railroad tracks fanned out from Chicago across the Midwest. Trains left Chicago every day carrying goods from factories to small farming towns. The trains returned loaded with corn, wheat, and livestock for the big cities.

Today, railroads, highways, airports, rivers, and lakes move more people and goods into and out of Chicago than any other American city. Moving all these people and goods is a big business. O'Hare International Airport alone employs 50,000 workers. Someday, you might be one of them.

As an economist, I know how important transportation is to the economy of the Midwest. Last year, for example, my college buddy from Iowa sold his entire soy bean crop to a buyer in Japan. Without good transportation, how could he get his crop halfway around the world?

transportation hub a city that serves as a center for moving goods and people

Many products from the Midwest are shipped from O'Hare International Airport to places all over the world.

8.9 Chicago's Wrigley Field

This has to be the best view in the world—at least for a baseball fan. We are looking at Wrigley Field, home of the Chicago Cubs.

Sports are popular in the Midwest. The first professional baseball team played not far from here, in Cincinnati, Ohio.

As a kid, I listened to the Cubs play baseball on the radio. The Cubs never won a championship. But I still became a big fan. Now that I live in Chicago, I love watching the Cubs play at Wrigley Field.

Wrigley Field is a special place for people who like baseball. It is the second-oldest baseball park in America. A lot of historic events have happened here. The most famous may be Babe Ruth's "called shot" during Game 3 of the 1932 World Series. The story is that Ruth pointed to the bleachers when he was up at bat. Then, on the next pitch, he hit a home run to that very spot. I wish I'd been there to see it.

Baseball is a popular sport in the Midwest thanks to many historic games played at Chicago's Wrigley Field.

People from all over the world come to the Midwest to visit the Mall of America.

8.10 Minnesota's Amazing Mall of America

Our last stop is the Mall of America in Bloomington, Minnesota. This is the largest indoor shopping mall in the United States.

The nation's first covered mall was built in the Midwest in 1956. Its purpose was to make shopping a pleasant experience, no matter what the weather.

People in the Midwest are always watching the weather. In winter, storms called *blizzards* bring heavy snow and freezing winds. Spring brings hailstorms that drop hailstones, or lumps of ice, instead of rain. Spring also begins tornado season. A tornado is a swirling windstorm that destroys almost everything in its path.

Indoor malls protect shoppers from the weather. They also give customers lots of choices about what to buy.

The Mall of America has more than 520 stores! If you spent just 10 minutes in each one, it would take you four days and three nights to visit the entire mall. This is without taking time to eat in one of the 50 restaurants, visit any of the 14 movie theaters, or play in the amusement park.

8.11 Chapter Summary

When we began, I asked you why the Midwest is called "America's Breadbasket." Midwestern farmers grow a lot of the wheat we use to make bread. Kansas grows the most wheat. North Dakota, South Dakota, Minnesota, Ohio, Illinois, and Nebraska also produce large wheat crops. This is how the Midwest earned the nickname.

Why do we also call the Midwest "America's Heartland"? There are many answers to this question. One answer looks at geography. The Midwest lies at the heart, or center, of the United States.

Another answer looks at history. The Midwest is where pioneers began their westward journeys. It is where Native Americans fought bravely to defend their land. This is also where America's professional sport of baseball began.

A third answer looks at economics. The Midwest is a center for both farming and industry. From popcorn to cars, many products you use every day come from America's economic heartland.

Our planes are about to land. Thank you very much for coming on my tour. I hope you can return to the Midwest soon.

This machine harvests snap beans. One mechanical harvester can replace about 100 people picking beans by hand.

chapter 9

Agricultural Changes in the Nation's Breadbasket

9.1 Introduction

"Tickle the land with a hoe," boasted a midwestern farmer in the 1800s, "and the crop will laugh to the harvest."

Midwesterners liked to brag about their farms. They bragged about the farm boy who got stuck on the top of a cornstalk because the corn grew faster than he could climb. They boasted about pumpkins so large that cows could live inside them. They even told stories about giant water-melons. These melons were so big they had to be pulled out of fields on sleds.

This much is true: the Midwest has some of the richest soil anywhere. And many crops grow well there.

Still, farming in the Midwest has never been as easy as tickling the land with a hoe. The first farmers to settle there worked hard to survive. Much has changed since then. But midwestern farmers still have to work hard to survive.

Farm Equipment Through the Centuries

At first, farmers avoided these grassy areas. They thought nothing but grass could grow there. But they quickly learned that the prairie soil was deep and rich.

9.2 Farming in the Midwest in 1800

In the year 1800, almost all Americans lived on farms. About 90 out of every 100 people in America lived on a farm. Most farms had only as much land as one family could plow and plant in a year. This was about 50 acres.

Most of these farms were east of the Appalachian Mountains. However, settlers were beginning to cross the mountains looking for new land to farm. By 1810, more than a million Americans lived west of the Appalachians.

Farmers settled first in the states of Ohio, Michigan, and Indiana. This part of the country is called the Central Plains. At that time, it was covered with forests.

As farmers moved west into the states of Illinois and Wisconsin, the forest grew thinner. Patches of prairie appeared. A prairie is an area of flat or gently rolling land that is covered with grasses and wildflowers.

Clearing forests and prairies for planting was hard work. Most farmers were doing well to raise enough food for their families.

9.3 Farming Tools in 1800

The tools farmers used in 1800 were simple. They used axes to cut down trees. Some trees were sawn into logs to build log cabins. Others were made into fences or furniture.

A plow with an iron blade was used to prepare soil for planting. As this blade was dragged across a field, it dug a long groove called a **furrow**.

If they were lucky, farmers had a pair of oxen to pull their plows. Even then, plowing was slow work. The thick prairie soil stuck to the iron blades. Farmers had to stop every few steps to scrape dirt from their plows.

Farmers planted their crops by hand. They walked up and down their fields, dropping seeds into the fresh furrows. They hoped the seeds would take root in this loose soil.

Farmers used a **scythe**—a curved knife on a long handle—to harvest their grain crops. Later they threshed the grain by beating it with a **flail**. **Threshing** separates the seeds of grain from the rest of the plant.

With these tools, a farmer had to work about 300 hours to raise 100 bushels of wheat. To raise this much wheat, he had to plow, plant, and harvest 5 acres of land.

furrow a groove made in the soil for planting seeds
scythe a curved knife on a long handle used for cutting grain
flail a tool for beating harvested grain
thresh to separate grain seeds from the rest of the plant

Farmers often hired a team of men with scythes to help harvest fields of wheat.

9.4 The Family Farm in 1800

The first farmhouse most families built was a log cabin. The typical cabin had one main room and perhaps a sleeping loft. There was a stone fireplace for cooking and heating. The main room was furnished with a table and a few stools.

Cabins were gloomy inside. Greased paper covered the small windows. At night, the only light came from the fire and smelly lamps that burned grease. Farm families went to bed early. Most slept on mattresses stuffed with oak leaves under quilts made from scraps of cloth.

Farm families raised almost all of their own food. They planted vegetable gardens and fruit orchards. They kept cows for milk, butter, and cheese. They raised chickens for eggs and hogs for meat. They raised sheep for wool, which they made into clothes.

Farm families faced many hardships. Often they did not have enough to eat. Wolves ate their chickens and hogs. Rabbits and deer raided their gardens. Squirrels and raccoons robbed their cornfields.

Disease could strike at any time. Injuries were common, as well. Women hurt themselves cooking over open fires. Men hurt themselves in the fields. With no doctors nearby, farm families did their best to care for themselves.

A farmyard in 1800 was a busy, noisy place. How many kinds of animals can you see in this picture?

9.5 Farming in the Midwest in 1900

In the year 1900, less than half of all Americans lived on farms. About 40 out of every 100 people in America lived on a farm. Most farms were three times the size of farms 100 years earlier. The average farm was 150 acres in size.

The first farmers on the plains worked hard to be self-sufficient. Being **self-sufficient** means doing everything for yourself. They raised their own food and made their own clothes. These self-sufficient farmers didn't make much money. But they didn't need much money, either.

By 1900, farms covered the Midwest. No longer did farmers plant just enough land to feed their families. Instead, they raised large crops of grain and great herds of animals.

Farmers on the Central Plains raised corn, pigs, and dairy cows. On the Great Plains, they raised wheat, cattle, and sheep. They sold their crops and livestock for cash.

With more money, farmers could buy more land. They could purchase machines to help them work that land. And they could buy the wonderful new goods coming out of American factories—such as iron stoves, sewing machines, telephones, and pianos.

A country store in 1900 sold just about everything a farmer might need.

self-sufficient doing everything necessary to take care of yourself

A combine harvester and thresher was a very heavy piece of equipment. This photo was taken in a wheatfield near Moro, Oregon, in the 1890s. Notice how many horses were needed to pull the combine.

9.6 Farm Tools in 1900

During the 1800s, Americans had invented many new farm tools. Many of these tools were pulled through fields by teams of horses.

The most important new tool for prairie farmers was the steel plow. A man named John Deere invented it in 1837. Deere's plows were made with steel blades instead of blades made of iron. Steel blades were sharper and smoother than iron blades. As a result, steel plows could cut through the thick prairie soil far more easily than the old iron plows.

Another new tool was a grain-cutting machine called a **reaper**. A man named Cyrus McCormick invented it in 1834. A farmer could cut much more grain with McCormick's reaper than with a scythe.

Other machines followed the reaper. One was the horse-drawn seed drill. This machine planted seeds much faster than a farmer could by hand. Another was the horse-drawn combine. A **combine** cut and threshed a field of grain all at once.

New tools helped midwestern farmers grow more food with less effort. By 1900, a farmer needed just 50 hours to raise 100 bushels of wheat. It took this long to plant and harvest 5 acres using horse-drawn machines.

reaper a machine for cutting grain

combine a machine pulled by horses for cutting and threshing grain

9.7 The Family Farm in 1900

The first farm homes on the plains were tents, log cabins, and soddies. Soddies were houses made of blocks of **sod,** or dirt mixed with grass roots. When it rained, soddies dripped mud. "Life is too short," wrote one woman, "to be spent under a sod roof."

As soon as farm families had some money saved, they built houses made of sawn lumber. The typical farmhouse had lots of windows and a big porch. The largest room was the kitchen. Few farmhouses had bathrooms. Instead, families used an outhouse built behind the main house.

Only the richest farmers could afford such wonders as electricity and running water. Most farm families used candles or oil lamps for lighting. They cooked on wood-burning iron stoves. They used hand pumps to draw water from wells.

Everybody worked. Men plowed, planted, and harvested crops. Women cooked, cleaned, and cared for the children. In summer, farm women spent hours canning food from their gardens. **Canning** is a method of preserving food by cooking and sealing it in cans or jars.

Every child had chores, as well. Children helped by chopping wood, drawing water, and weeding the garden. They also gathered eggs, milked cows, and fed the animals.

sod a mixture of dirt and roots of grass used to build sod houses

canning preserving food by cooking and sealing it in cans or jars

This sod house was in Custer County, Nebraska. The family was photographed next to their well.

Crop dusters are airplanes that fly low over a farm, spraying pesticides over fields of plants.

9.8 Farming in the Midwest Today

By the year 2000, very few Americans lived and worked on farms. Only 2 out of every 100 people in America lived on a farm. Farms were almost 10 times the size of farms 200 years earlier. The average farm was 450 acres in size.

Farming in the 21st century is a big business. Most farms are still owned and run by families. But some are owned by large companies. These companies hire farmworkers to work their land.

Farming in the Midwest has changed in many ways over the past 100 years. Today, most farmwork is done with machines. Most farmers add **fertilizers** to soil to make plants grow better. Some fertilizers are natural products. Others are made from chemicals. Farmers also use chemicals to kill insects and other pests that attack their crops. These products are called **pesticides**.

These changes have helped farmers grow more food than ever before. But they have also created new problems. Chemicals used on crops can be harmful to other living things. For example, fertilizers and pesticides wash into rivers. There, they can kill fish and other wildlife.

fertilizer a substance added to soil to improve plant growth

pesticide a substance used on crops to kill insects and other pests

9.9 Farm Tools Today

By 2000, most of the work of plowing, planting, and picking crops was done by machines. The power for these machines comes from gasoline engines.

The most important new farm tool of the last 100 years is the tractor. Tractors are used in two ways on farms. One is to pull heavy loads. A modern tractor can pull more weight than 100 horses. The other is to power other farm equipment. Farmers use tractors to power plows, seed drills, and machines that harvest their crops.

For dairy farmers, no tool has been more useful than the milking machine. Before milking machines, dairy farmers had to milk each cow by hand. This was slow work. Milking machines allow a farmer to milk many cows at once. As a result, dairy farms are much larger today than they were in 1900.

New tools helped midwestern farmers grow more food on less land. In 1800, a farmer needed 5 acres to grow 100 bushels of wheat. By 2000, the same amount of wheat could be grown on just 3 acres.

New machines also cut the time necessary to raise 100 bushels of wheat. It now takes under 4 hours. In 1800, it took 300 hours to raise that much wheat.

Compare this photo of a tractor pulling a combine to the photo on page 104 of the horse-drawn combine.

Farm auctions are like huge yard sales at which a farmer's equipment is sold to pay the farm's bills.

9.10 The Family Farm Today

Throughout our history, farms have grown year after year. As the nation expanded westward, the number of farms increased. By the 1920s, there were more than 6 million farms in the United States.

In the 1930s, hard times hit the family farm. Crop prices fell so low farmers could not make any money. Then a long drought struck the Midwest. With no rain, fields turned to dust. Many families gave up farming.

Since then, farmers have seen good times and bad. But the number of family farms has dropped year by year. Today, there are barely 2 million farms left in the United States.

The families on these farms live like most other Americans. They buy their clothes in department stores. They send their children to school and college. They watch television in the evenings.

Every year, more people leave farming. Some get tired of the hard work. Others don't like the loneliness of farm life. But most leave for one simple reason. They can't make enough money farming to pay their bills.

9.11 Chapter Summary

As you have seen, farming in the Midwest has changed a lot in 200 years. In 1800, farmers worked the land with their own muscles and hand tools. Most could not raise much more food than they needed to feed their families.

Today, farmers work the land with powerful tractors and machines. They also use fertilizers to grow more food on every acre of land. As a result, one farmer can raise enough food to feed many families.

In 1800, farm families grew or made almost everything they needed. They bought very little. Today, farmers grow large crops for sale. With the money they make from their crops, they buy what they need in stores.

Some things have not changed much in 200 years. Farming was hard work in 1800. It is still hard work today. In 1800, everyone in the family helped out on the farm. That is still true on most family farms today.

One other thing has not changed in the past 200 years. Farming was a risky business in 1800. Lots of things could go wrong. It is still a risky business today. But for those who love to work the land, there is no better way of life.

chapter 10

A Big Rig Tour of the Southwest

10.1 Introduction

Welcome to the Southwest. My name is Mr. Nakai. I will be your guide this week.

Let me tell you a little about myself. I am a Navaho Indian. Until I retired last year, I was a truck driver. I drove my big rig—that's what truckers call their trucks—all over the Southwest. I know this region like the back of my hand.

When I was asked to lead this tour, I thought about how I could make it really special. Then it hit me! I'm a trucker. Why not take you on a truck tour? My big rig holds only three people. But some of my trucking buddies offered to help out. Together, we rounded up enough trucks to take your whole class.

The view from high up in a big rig can't be beat. So pick a truck, buckle your seat belt, and let's go.

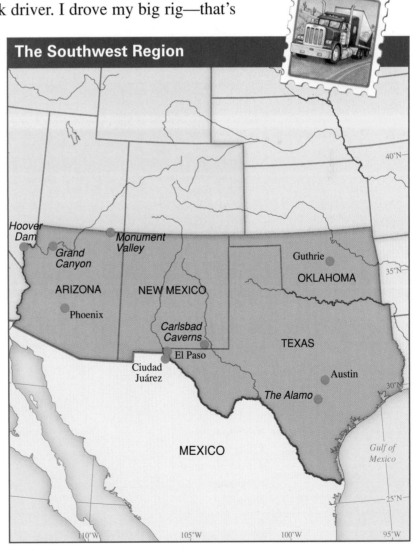

The Southwest Region

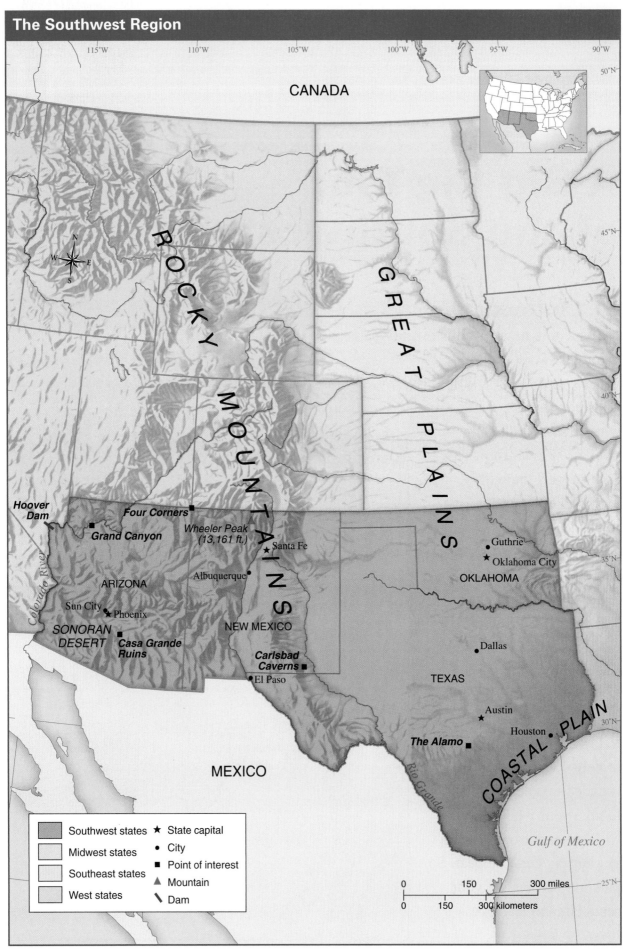

CANADA

115°W
110°W
105°W
100°W
95°W
90°W

50°N

45°N

R O C K Y

G R E A T

40°N

M O U N T A I N S

P L A I N S

Hoover
Dam

Four Corners

35°N

Grand Canyon

Wheeler Peak
(13,161 ft.)

Santa Fe

Guthrie

Oklahoma City

Albuquerque

OKLAHOMA

ARIZONA

Colorado River

Sun City

Phoenix

NEW MEXICO

SONORAN
DESERT

Casa Grande
Ruins

Dallas

Carlsbad
Caverns

El Paso

TEXAS

Austin

MEXICO

The Alamo

Houston

COASTAL PLAIN

Rio Grande

30°N

Gulf of Mexico

25°N

■ Southwest states	★ State capital	
☐ Midwest states	● City	
☐ Southeast states	■ Point of interest	
☐ West states	▲ Mountain	
	＼ Dam	

0   150   300 miles

0   150   300 kilometers

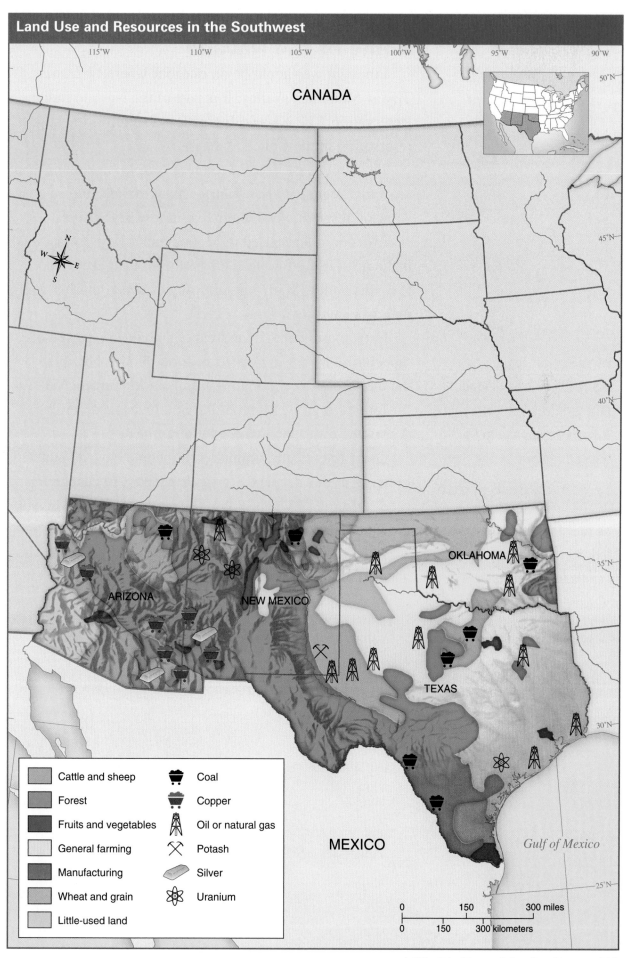

Land Use and Resources in the Southwest

CANADA

115°W 110°W 105°W 100°W 95°W 90°W

50°N

45°N

40°N

35°N

OKLAHOMA

ARIZONA

NEW MEXICO

30°N

TEXAS

MEXICO

Gulf of Mexico

25°N

	Cattle and sheep		Coal
	Forest		Copper
	Fruits and vegetables		Oil or natural gas
	General farming		Potash
	Manufacturing		Silver
	Wheat and grain		Uranium
	Little-used land		

0   150   300 miles

0   150   300 kilometers

10.2 Monument Valley: Home of the Navaho

I thought we should begin our tour where I began. This is Monument Valley. It is part of the Navaho Indian Reservation. The Navaho Indian Reservation is the largest reservation in the United States.

The Southwest is home to more Native Americans than any other region of the country. Many Indians live and work on reservations. Others live in towns and cities.

I was born and raised in Monument Valley. To me, this is the most beautiful place on Earth. Moviemakers also love this valley. Many western movies and television commercials have been filmed here.

Look closely at this landscape. Do you see those flat-topped hills? They are called **mesas**. Notice how bare the mesas are. Not enough rain falls in Monument Valley for forests to grow. Much of the Southwest is desert. A **desert** is dry land where little rain falls.

Over time, plants, animals, and people have all adapted to living in this dry land. To **adapt** means to change in order to survive. The Navaho, for example, learned how to grow corn and raise sheep with little rainfall.

As we move on, look for other ways that people have adapted to living in the desert.

mesa a flat-topped hill
desert an area of land that receives very little rain
adapt to change to fit new conditions

The rock formations in Monument Valley are made of shale and sandstone.

10.3 Phoenix, Arizona: America's Hottest City

This is Phoenix, Arizona, America's hottest large city. During the summer, temperatures here can soar to 115 degrees Fahrenheit.

A hundred years ago, Phoenix was a small town. Not many people wanted to move to Arizona in those days. Folks said it was too hot, dry, and lonely here. What I call the three "A's" changed their minds.

The first "A" was air conditioners. These machines use electricity to cool the air in a room. Air conditioning lets people live in comfort no matter how hot the day is.

The second "A" was aqueducts. An **aqueduct** is a large pipe or canal that moves water over a long distance. Aqueducts are used in the Southwest to move water from lakes and rivers to farms and cities. Aqueducts make it possible to have green lawns in Phoenix.

The third "A" was automobiles. Travel in the Southwest used to be hard and even dangerous. A traveler who got stuck in the desert could die of thirst.

Cars, along with good roads, made travel safer and easier. Folks began to come to the Phoenix area as tourists. Some liked the hot, dry weather so much that they came back to live here. Since 1940, Phoenix has grown at an amazing rate.

With a population of more than 1,320,000 people, Phoenix is the sixth-largest U.S. city.

aqueduct a pipe or canal for carrying a large quantity of water

10.4 Hoover Dam: A Concrete Marvel

Hoover Dam is on the borders of the states of Arizona and Nevada.

You are looking at one of America's greatest manufactured structures: Hoover Dam. A **dam** is a wall built across a river.

Hoover Dam was built for two main reasons. The first reason was to control flooding on the Colorado River. The dam slows the rush of water down the river during flood times. The second reason was to store water. Water stored behind Hoover Dam flows through aqueducts to farms and cities.

Hoover Dam was built more than 60 years ago. At that time, nobody had ever built such a huge dam.

Lots of people said it couldn't be done. Some said the Colorado River could never be stopped long enough to build a dam. Others did not think a dam could be made strong enough to hold back so much water. My dad helped prove these people wrong! He helped build Hoover Dam.

dam a wall built across a river to stop the flow of water

My dad was full of facts about Hoover Dam. He told me that there is enough concrete in the dam to pave a two-lane road from California to Florida. He said that the lake behind the dam holds enough water to flood the entire state of New York with one foot of water. That's a lot of concrete holding back a lot of water.

10.5 The Grand Canyon: Arizona's World-Famous Wonder

Wow—what a view! You are looking into the Grand Canyon. This is the most famous natural feature in the United States—maybe even the world!

A **canyon** is a deep, narrow valley with steep sides. There are many canyons in the Southwest. But this one is the grandest of them all.

The Grand Canyon is about 277 miles long and 1 mile deep. It is so deep that the top and bottom have different weather. It can be cold here on top and hot down below. It is so deep that when I stand here on the rim, I sometimes see eagles flying below me.

Native Americans known as the Havasupai live at the bottom of the Grand Canyon. According to Havasupai legend, the canyon was formed when a flood covered the world. To end the flood, a god dug a hole in the earth. The floodwater rushed down the hole, carving out the Grand Canyon as it went.

Scientists tell a different story. They say the Grand Canyon began to form about 10 million years ago. It has been carved slowly out of the earth by water and wind. The Grand Canyon is still growing today, even while we are here looking at it.

The rocks of the Grand Canyon tell us what the world was like hundreds of millions of years ago.

cave a natural underground hole

cavern a large cave

Limestone and water created the formations in these caverns.

10.6 Big Rooms and Bats in Carlsbad Caverns, New Mexico

At most national parks, the big attractions are found above the ground. Not here! At Carlsbad Caverns National Park in New Mexico, the show takes place underground. More than 85 caves and caverns lie beneath this park. A **cave** is natural hole found under the earth. A **cavern** is a large cave.

According to local legend, a cowboy named Jim White found Carlsbad Caverns. One evening, White saw what looked like a plume of smoke rising into the sky. Turns out that smoke was a cloud of bats flying out of a cave entrance.

A bat is a small, furry animal. It looks like a mouse with wings. Hundreds of thousands of bats sleep in the caverns during the day. At night they leave in a great, whirring cloud to hunt for food. If you come to the entrance at sunset, you may see them take flight. It's a pretty sight.

More than half a million visitors tour Carlsbad Caverns each year. One of the most popular stops is a huge chamber known as the Big Room. The Big Room is 25 stories high and a third of a mile wide. It could hold 14 football fields and still have space left over.

10.7 El Paso and Ciudad Juárez: Two Cities, Two Countries, One Border

We are at the border between the United States and Mexico. A **border** is a line that people agree on to separate two places. The border between the United States and Mexico is a river known as the Rio Grande.

The Rio Grande separates two countries. It also divides two cities. El Paso, Texas, an American city, lies north of border. Ciudad Juárez, a Mexican city, lies south of the border.

When I began driving trucks 30 years ago, El Paso and Juárez were sleepy little border towns. There weren't many people or trucks here then. Today more than 2 million people live here. And the place is crawling with trucks.

The reason for this change is pretty simple. American businesses have built hundreds of factories in Juárez. These factories, called *maquiladoras,* assemble all kinds of goods. The goods are then trucked across the border for sale in the United States.

Americans build factories across the border because Mexican workers will work for much lower pay than American workers. This reduces their cost of doing business.

Mexicans move to the border because that's where the jobs are. A maquiladora job may not pay a lot, but it beats no job at all.

The Rio Grande forms the border between the United States and Mexico. The river begins in the mountains of Colorado and Mexico.

border a boundary that separates two places

The Alamo was built mainly from adobe (bricks made of earth and straw) and stone.

10.8 San Antonio, Texas: Home of the Alamo

Welcome to San Antonio, Texas. San Antonio is famous for its missions. A **mission** is a Spanish settlement where priests taught Native Americans the Christian religion.

San Antonio's missions were built in the early 1700s. At that time, Texas was a colony of Spain. Later, Texas became part of Mexico.

The Alamo is San Antonio's most famous mission. More than two and a half million people visit the Alamo every year. They come to see where a small band of men fought and died so that Texas might be free.

In 1836, Americans living in Texas declared their independence from Mexican rule. Mexico sent 6,000 troops to Texas to crush this rebellion. A **rebellion** is an armed fight against one's government.

A band of 188 Texas freedom fighters gathered at the Alamo. Their goal was to stop the Mexican army there. Instead, Mexican forces captured the mission. Then they killed each and every one of its defenders.

News of the killings at the Alamo outraged Americans. Thousands picked up their guns and headed to Texas to join the rebellion. Their battle cry was, "Remember the Alamo!"

Texas won its independence in 1836. Nine years later, it joined the United States as the 28th state.

mission a Spanish settlement in the United States for teaching Christianity

rebellion an armed fight against a government

10.9 Austin: The Capital of Texas

This is Austin, the capital of Texas. A **capital** is a city where the government of a country or state is located. The government of Texas is located in Austin.

Like our national government, state governments have three branches. The legislative branch is the state legislature. The Texas legislature meets in the building you see here with the large dome on top.

State legislatures make laws for all the people in a state. Most of the traffic laws in each state are passed by the state legislature. As a truck driver, I had to know and obey all those laws.

State legislatures decide how much people must pay in taxes to the state. They also decide how that money will be spent. Truckers always want state legislatures to spend more money on improving roads.

The executive branch is headed by the state governor. It's the governor's job to make sure that all the laws passed by the state legislature are carried out.

State courts make up the judicial branch. State courts judge people who are accused of breaking state laws. If a person is found guilty of breaking a law, the courts decide how that person should be punished.

I'm proud to say that, in all my years of trucking, I never had to go to court for breaking a traffic law.

This famous Austin landmark is the largest of the U.S. state capitol buildings.

capital a city where the government of a country or state is located

10.10 Guthrie, Oklahoma: Center of the Land Rush

Most of the Southwest was settled slowly, over time. Guthrie, Oklahoma, was settled in a day.

For many years, the U.S. government kept Oklahoma closed to everyone but Native Americans. Then, in 1889, it decided to open 2 million acres of land to settlement. This area was to be given away in a one-day land rush. The first person to reach and claim a piece of land on that day would receive it.

On April 22, 1889, between 50,000 and 100,000 people gathered at the starting line for the land rush. Most were European Americans. About 10,000 were African Americans. Black or white, everyone wanted the same thing: free land.

At noon, a shot rang out. The rush was on! People raced off in wagons, on horses, and on foot. In a few hours, every inch of land was taken.

Not everyone waited for the land rush to begin. Some settlers "jumped the gun" and entered the area sooner than the government allowed. One of these "sooners" was found tending a garden full of vegetables. Oklahoma's soil was so rich, he claimed, that the plants had all sprouted up that day.

Guthrie was born during the land rush. At noon, Guthrie wasn't much more than a patch of grass. Six hours later, the town had 10,000 people.

The army held back the crowds until a pistol shot signaled the beginning of the land rush.

10.11 Chapter Summary

My trucking buddies and I hope you enjoyed your big rig tour of the Southwest.

On the way back, I asked the children in my truck what words they would use to describe the Southwest. The first word they came up with was *big*. This is a big region. And you saw a lot of it.

Their next two words were *hot* and *dry*. Much of the Southwest is desert. Plants, animals, and people all have to adapt to its hot, dry climate to survive.

Over time, the way people adapt to the desert has changed. The Navaho came here hundreds of years ago. They adapted by learning how to grow corn and raise sheep. People coming here today adapt in different ways. They look to air conditioning, aqueducts, and automobiles to help them survive.

The last word the children chose was *beautiful*. I asked which places seemed beautiful to them. "Monument Valley," they answered, "along with the Grand Canyon and Carlsbad Caverns." After thinking about this some more, one of the kids added, "I think Hoover Dam is beautiful, too."

My dad would have liked that answer. He would have liked it a lot.

Hoover Dam holds back the water of the Colorado river to make Lake Mead.

chapter 11

A Case Study in Water Use: The Colorado River

11.1 Introduction

Many rivers flow through the United States. Few are as important as the Colorado River.

The people of the Southwest rely on the Colorado River for many things. The Colorado provides drinking water for 25 million people. It supplies water for more than 3 million acres of farmland. Dams on the river help produce much of the electricity used in the Southwest.

The Colorado River begins high in the Rocky Mountains. The beginning of a river is called its **source**. The Colorado wanders south and west down through some of the driest parts of the country. Then, it crosses into Mexico and ends in the Gulf of California. Its journey is 1,470 miles long.

Many smaller rivers flow into the Colorado. Rivers that join other rivers are called **tributaries**. Each tributary adds water and soil, called *silt,* to the Colorado. This silt gives the river its reddish-brown color.

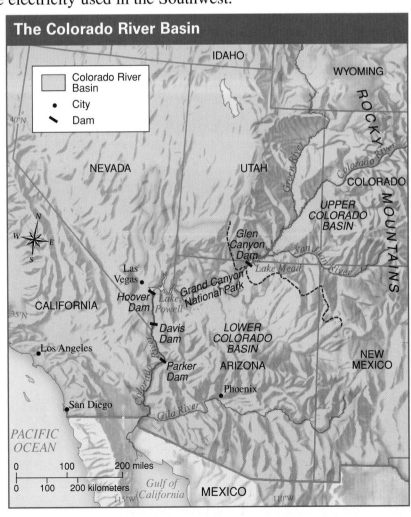

The Colorado River Basin

- Colorado River Basin
- • City
- ╲ Dam

IDAHO
WYOMING
NEVADA
UTAH
ROCKY MOUNTAINS
COLORADO
Green River
Colorado River
UPPER COLORADO BASIN
San Juan River
Glen Canyon Dam
Lake Mead
Las Vegas
Hoover Dam
Lake Powell
Grand Canyon National Park
CALIFORNIA
Davis Dam
LOWER COLORADO BASIN
NEW MEXICO
Los Angeles
Parker Dam
ARIZONA
Phoenix
San Diego
Gila River
PACIFIC OCEAN
0   100   200 miles
0   100   200 kilometers
Gulf of California
MEXICO

11.2 The First Settlers in the Colorado River Basin

Today, millions of people live in the Colorado River Basin. A **river basin** is the area around a river and its tributaries. Not that long ago, this area was an empty desert.

Two of the Native American groups that once made their homes in this dry region were the Anasazi and the Hohokam. The Anasazi lived in the Four Corners area. This is where the states of Arizona, New Mexico, Utah, and Colorado meet today. The Hohokam lived in Central Arizona.

The Anasazi and the Hohokam were farmers. They raised corn, beans, and squash in desert fields. Not enough rain fell to water their crops. So they built canals to carry water from rivers to their fields. Some Hohokam canals were so well built that they are still used today.

Around 1150, the Anasazi left their villages forever. A few hundred years later, the Hohokam also disappeared. The name Hohokam means "those who have gone."

Why did they leave? No one is sure. But the most likely answer is drought. A **drought** is a time when little or no rain falls. When no rain came and their rivers ran dry, the Anasazi and the Hohokam knew they had two choices. They could leave and live, or stay and die. They chose to leave their villages to live in other parts of the Southwest.

The Hohokam used simple tools to help build irrigation canals.

11.3 The River Is Explored

Spanish explorers were the first Europeans to visit the Southwest. In 1540, a Spanish soldier named Francisco Vásquez de Coronado led an army north from Mexico. Coronado was hoping to find cities made of gold in the Southwest. Instead, he found Native American villages built from mud and stone.

In their search for gold, some of Coronado's men discovered the Grand Canyon. From high up on the canyon rim, the river at the bottom looked like a trickling creek. They didn't even bother to give it a name.

Spanish settlers followed Coronado into the Southwest. Most lived by farming and ranching. These settlers finally named the muddy river flowing through the Grand Canyon. They called it the Colorado, which means "reddish color" in Spanish.

The Colorado River was not explored until 1869. That year, a man named John Wesley Powell and a crew of nine men floated down the Colorado in small boats. They were the first Americans to see the Grand Canyon from the bottom. The trip took three months.

At the end of his journey, Powell wrote a report on the Colorado River Basin. He said that the region was too dry for much settlement. He believed there just wasn't enough water for a large number of people.

In 1871, John Wesley Powell made a second trip down the Colorado in order to map the river.

11.4 The First Wave of Settlement

Powell's warning did not keep people from settling in the Colorado River Basin. Some of the newcomers were farmers. Like the Anasazi and the Hohokam, they found they could grow crops in the desert. They just had to bring a lot of water to their fields.

Other settlers became cattle and sheep ranchers. Sheep and cattle could live off plants that grew wild in the Southwest. But ranchers had to find drinking water for their animals. Some ranchers also needed water to raise crops of hay for their animals.

As the number of settlers grew, towns appeared in the basin. A few—such as Los Angeles, California, and Phoenix, Arizona—grew into cities. People living in these towns and cities needed water for drinking, washing, and watering their gardens.

Irrigation ditches bring water to this field of lettuce in New Mexico.

All of these people looked to the Colorado and its tributaries for their water needs.

11.5 Sharing the Water: The Colorado River Compact

At first, the Colorado River had enough water for everyone. Water was divided up following the law of "first in time, first in right." Those who settled first were first in line to draw water from the river. Those who came last were last in line.

This way of dividing water created a problem. Most of the first water users lived in California. This meant that California had the right to use almost all of the river's water. This didn't seem fair to other states in the river basin.

In 1922, the seven river basin states reached an agreement. This agreement is known as the Colorado River Compact. The compact divided the basin into two parts. The upper basin states are Wyoming, Utah, Colorado, and New Mexico. The lower basin states are Arizona, Nevada, and California. The compact gave each part of the basin an equal amount of water from the Colorado River.

The Colorado River Compact said nothing about Mexico. Water users there worried that there would be no water left by the time the river crossed the border. So, the United States signed a separate water agreement with Mexico. In it, the United States promised to leave some water in the Colorado River for Mexico.

The delegates from the seven basin states signed the Colorado River Compact at Bishop's Lodge, New Mexico, on November 24, 1922.

Hoover Dam spans the Colorado River between Nevada and Arizona. Millions of visitors come to the dam's reservoir every year to boat, fish, swim, hike, and camp. The reservoir is called Lake Mead.

11.6 Taming the River with Dams

The Colorado River Compact gave each state the right to part of the river's flow. But turning that right into a constant water supply was not easy. In wet years, the river flooded over its banks. In dry years, the river barely flowed.

The only way a state could get and keep its share of river water was to find a way to trap and store it. This meant building dams. A dam is a wall built across a river to hold back water. As water backs up behind a dam, it forms a reservoir. A **reservoir** is a place where water is stored.

Since the 1930s, 8 dams have been built on the Colorado River. Another 12 have been built on its tributaries. These dams have tamed the river. In wet years, they prevent flooding by not letting too much water flow down the river at one time. In dry years, their reservoirs provide water to farms and cities.

Each dam generates electricity. Water rushing through openings in a dam causes huge machines to spin. These machines are called *turbines*. The spinning turbines create electricity. This electricity is sold to help pay for the dams.

reservoir an area where water is stored

11.7 The Number of Water Users Grows and Grows

Soon, more people moved to the river basin. There were more and more new houses year after year. Still, the Colorado River provided water and electricity for everyone. Who are these water users?

The largest group is made up of families like yours. People need water to drink, wash clothes, shower, and flush toilets. Did you know that one load of laundry uses 35 to 50 gallons of water?

Farmers and ranchers are major water users. A farmer uses 8 gallons of water to grow one tomato. A rancher uses about 600 gallons of water to raise the beef for one hamburger.

Businesses are major water users. A soft drink company uses 16 gallons of water to produce one can of soda. A clothing company needs 1,800 gallons of water to make one pair of jeans from cotton.

Miners are major water users. Gold, iron, copper, coal, and uranium are found in the Colorado River Basin. Miners use large amounts of water to wash these valuable ores from the soil.

So far, the Colorado River has met the needs of these water users. But, as more people move into the basin, there may not be enough water for everyone.

Families can help save water by washing only full loads of laundry.

11.8 Wildlife Water Users

People are not the only water users in the Colorado River Basin. Mammals, birds, fish, and other animals also need the river.

The taming of the river has hurt wildlife by destroying their habitats. A **habitat** is the place where an animal lives in nature. The natural habitat of fish, for example, is water.

Dams built on the Colorado have turned parts of the river into reservoirs. Beaver, otters, and other animals once lived along these parts of the river. Now their habitats are deep under water.

Dams also have changed the water in the river. Before dams were built, the river water was muddy and warm much of the year. The river's water level was at its high point in spring. Today the water released from a dam is clear and cold. Water is highest now in summer. That is when farmers and cities need water the most. These changes have hurt fish and other wildlife.

Today, dam operators are trying to help wildlife by releasing more water in spring. But this change means less water for people during the summer months.

habitat the place where an animal lives in nature

Mayflies, trout, lizards, and owls make their homes along the Colorado. So do thousands of other animals. What kinds of animals might live along this stretch of the river?

11.9 Is There Enough Water for Everyone?

The Colorado River Compact was based on the belief that $17\frac{1}{2}$ million acre-feet of water flow down the river each year. An acre-foot is the amount of water it would take to cover an acre of land with one foot of water. (An acre is about the size of a football field.)

This is how all that water was divided:

- *Upper basin states:* $7\frac{1}{2}$ million acre-feet
- *Lower basin states:* $7\frac{1}{2}$ million acre-feet
- *Mexico:* $1\frac{1}{2}$ million acre-feet
- *Total:* $16\frac{1}{2}$ million acre-feet

If the same amount of water flowed every year, this plan would work. But the river does not always carry this much water. In wet years, the flow may rise to over 20 million acre-feet. In dry years, it may fall below 10 million acre-feet. And there are more dry than wet years in the Colorado River Basin.

An acre-foot of water is about 326,000 gallons. This may sound like a lot, but it's not. A family of four uses 1 acre-foot of water each year. A farmer uses 3 acre-feet to water just one acre of land.

As more people settle in the Colorado River Basin, there may not be enough water for everyone.

About 90 percent of the water used in Las Vegas and the surrounding areas comes from the Colorado River.

Communities across the country are finding new ways to save water. You can help, too, by reporting leaky faucets at school and broken sprinklers around your city.

conservation the careful use of a resource
wastewater water that has been used

11.10 Meeting Future Water Needs

In the future, water users in the Colorado River Basin may face shortages. There are only two ways to solve this problem. One is to increase the supply of water. In the past, this was done by building dams. But most of the best places for dams have already been used. And now we know that dams hurt the natural environment.

The other solution is to use less water. This is called **conservation**. Conservation is the careful use of a resource. It sounds easy, but it's not. Using less water takes planning. It also takes new ways of thinking and new inventions.

Conservation efforts are already being made. For example, all new homes in the basin are built with low-flow toilets. These toilets use less than two gallons with each flush. Older toilets use up to seven gallons per flush.

The people of the United States are finding new ways to conserve water. For example, many cities are recycling the water that goes down the drain every day. This water is called **wastewater**. Cities collect and treat wastewater. They use the treated wastewater to water parks and golf courses.

11.11 Chapter Summary

If John Wesley Powell could see the Colorado River today, he would be amazed. The river he explored ran free from the Rocky Mountains to the Gulf of California.

Today, giant dams slow the river's rush to the sea. Those dams have changed the Colorado in ways Powell could never have imagined.

When Powell explored the Colorado River, no one lived on the land it flowed through. Today more than 25 million people live in the Colorado River Basin. Powell would be surprised to see so many people. He would also be surprised to find farms and cities blooming in the desert.

Before leaving, Powell might once again issue a report. Water is precious, he might tell us. More precious than gold. So use the river's gift of water wisely. It is, after all, the gift of life.

It takes a lot of water to keep a golf course green, especially in the desert. Many new businesses in the Colorado River Basin today are finding ways to conserve water.

A Van and Airplane Tour of the West

12.1 Introduction

Aloha! My name is Ms. Yoshida. I will be your guide for our tour of the West. As you can probably tell from my greeting, I was born and raised in Hawaii. *Aloha* is used for both "hello" and "goodbye" in the Hawaiian language.

I am a college student here on the mainland. My main interests are political science and government. Someday I hope to be elected to the United States Congress.

On school breaks, I work as a tour guide. It's a great job. I get to meet all kinds of people while seeing cool places. Whenever we visit someplace new, I want you to think about two questions: What first attracted people to this place? And why are people still coming here today?

For most of our tour, we will travel in vans. But we will also fly in airplanes to two stops.

Do you hear that honk? That means it's time for us to hit the road.

The West Region

A Van and Airplane Tour of the West   137

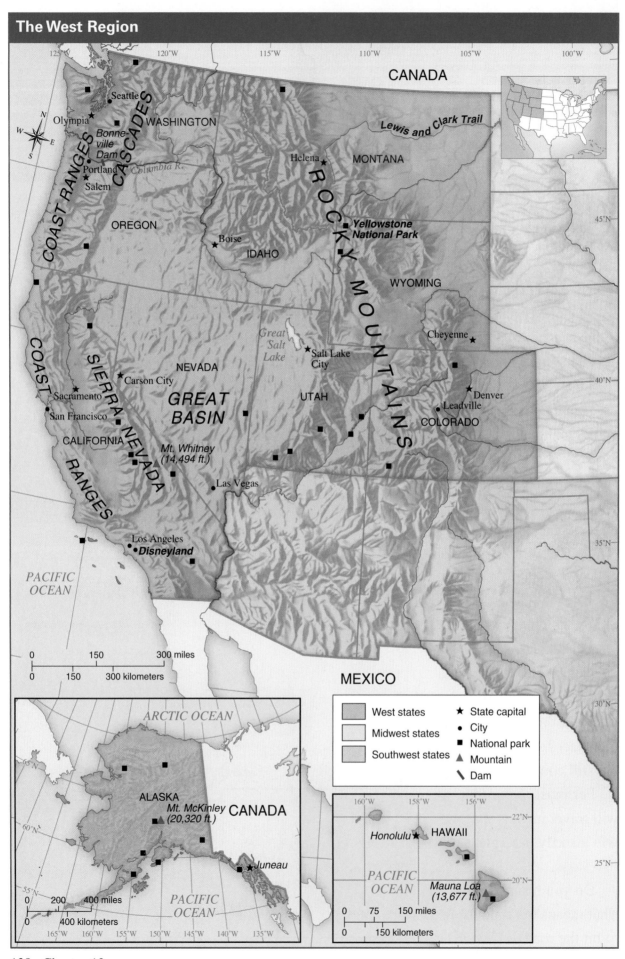

The West Region

CANADA

125°W 120°W 115°W 110°W 105°W 100°W

Seattle
Olympia ★
WASHINGTON
CASCADES
COAST RANGES
Bonneville Dam
Columbia R.
Portland ●
Salem ★
OREGON
Boise ★
IDAHO

Lewis and Clark Trail

Helena ★
MONTANA

Yellowstone National Park

ROCKY MOUNTAINS

WYOMING

45°N

Cheyenne ★

Great Salt Lake

Salt Lake City ★

NEVADA
Carson City ★
Sacramento ★
San Francisco ●
CALIFORNIA
SIERRA NEVADA
COAST RANGES

GREAT BASIN

UTAH

40°N

Denver ★
Leadville ●
COLORADO

Mt. Whitney ▲ (14,494 ft.)

Las Vegas ●

Los Angeles ●
● Disneyland

35°N

PACIFIC OCEAN

MEXICO

30°N

West states	★ State capital
Midwest states	● City
Southwest states	■ National park
	▲ Mountain
	＼ Dam

ARCTIC OCEAN

ALASKA
Mt. McKinley ▲ (20,320 ft.)
CANADA
Juneau ★
PACIFIC OCEAN

0 200 400 miles
0 400 kilometers

165°W 160°W 155°W 150°W 145°W 140°W 135°W

160°W 158°W 156°W
Honolulu ★ HAWAII
22°N
PACIFIC OCEAN
25°N
Mauna Loa (13,677 ft.)
20°N
0 75 150 miles
0 150 kilometers

0 150 300 miles
0 150 300 kilometers

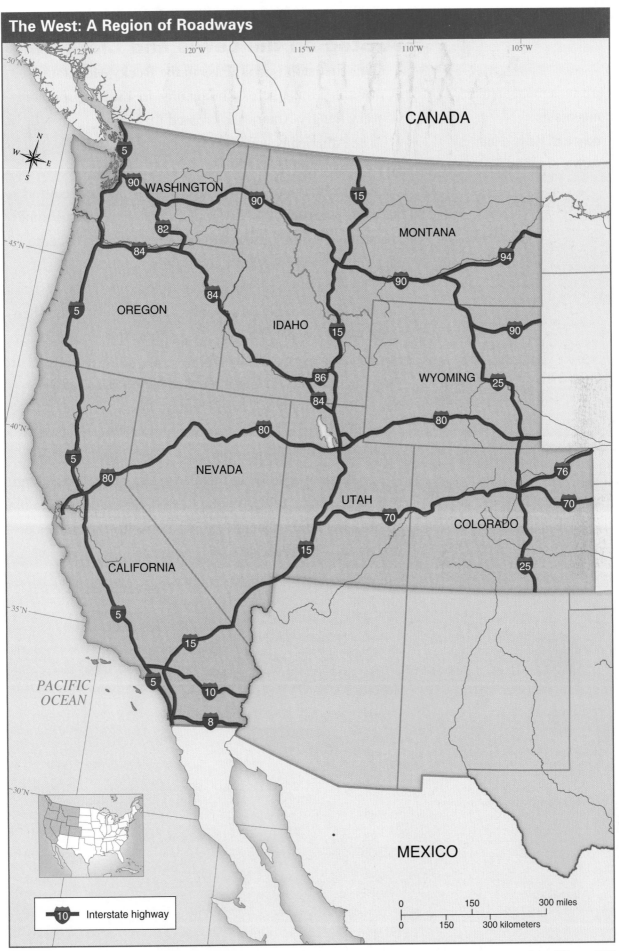

12.2 Lolo Pass, Montana: A Stop on the Lewis and Clark Trail

Our first stop is Lolo Pass in the Rocky Mountains. A **pass** is a route across mountains. In 1805, a group of 35 very hungry Americans crossed this pass.

The Americans were part of an expedition led by Meriwether Lewis and William Clark. An **expedition** is a journey with a purpose. The Lewis and Clark expedition had two purposes. The first was to find an all-water route from the Mississippi River to the Pacific Ocean. The travelers failed because such a route does not exist.

Their second purpose was to explore the lands west of the Mississippi. This Lewis and Clark did very well. Their maps and journals gave Americans their first good look at the region we now call the West.

When Lewis and Clark reached Lolo Pass, they were almost out of food. All they had left was a soup mix that everybody hated. The men survived by eating candles, bear oil, and two of their horses.

Today people come to this part of Montana to hike and fish. Some come to follow the Lewis and Clark Trail to the Pacific. Lucky for them, they don't have to eat candles or that awful soup to survive.

This old cabin lies along the Lewis and Clark National Historic Trail.

12.3 "Nature's Teakettles" in Wyoming's Yellowstone National Park

geyser a hot spring that throws jets of heated water and steam into the air

Lewis and Clark saw a lot of sights on their expedition. But they missed the geysers of Yellowstone National Park. A **geyser** is a hot spring that shoots boiling water and steam into the air. There are about 10,000 hot springs and geysers in Yellowstone.

Geysers are "nature's teakettles." Water is heated deep inside the earth. When the water gets hot enough, it hisses and boils just like a teakettle on a stove. What happens when this boiling water reaches Earth's surface? It shoots into the air. A geyser named Old Faithful erupts in a cloud of steam every 35 to 120 minutes.

Fur trappers were the first Americans to see Yellowstone. No one believed their stories of steaming springs. Later, a photographer took pictures of the geysers. People were impressed with the photographs. The land around the geysers became Yellowstone National Park. It is the first and oldest national park in the world.

With each eruption, Old Faithful spews more than 8,000 gallons of boiling water about 150 feet skyward.

Only 300 people visited Yellowstone the year it became a park. Today up to 4 million people come to Wyoming to visit the park each year. Visitors enjoy the beauty of Yellowstone's mountains and meadows.

This wooden entrance leads to a mine under a hillside in Leadville, Colorado.

12.4 Leadville, Colorado: The West's Richest Silver Mining Town

Welcome to historic Leadville, Colorado. We are looking at the entrance to an old mine.

Leadville is located in the Rocky Mountains. At 10,430 feet, it is our country's highest city. In the past, it was also the West's wildest and richest silver mining town.

Miners first came to this area looking for gold. They found some. But it was hard to separate gold from the local sand. Then, in 1878, a mineral expert took a closer look at that pesky sand. Guess what he found? The sand was rich in both lead and silver!

The discovery of silver brought good times to Leadville. The city grew rapidly as miners flocked to the area. Then, in 1893, the silver boom ended. For a time, it looked like Leadville would become an empty ghost town.

But Leadville was lucky. Other valuable minerals were found in this area. One is molybdenum. This metal is used in the production of high-strength steel. The town survived.

Today, Leadville is a tourist center. Some people come to learn about the history of this rich mining area. Others come to ski in winter or fish and hike in summer.

12.5 Sunny Southern California's Disneyland Park

Two really great things happened to me when I was in fourth grade. First, I was elected to my school's student council. That's how I got interested in government.

Second, my family visited Disneyland. The park seemed magical to me. At closing time, my parents had to drag me away.

Disneyland is in Southern California. It is part of a giant entertainment industry. This industry began by making movies. America's first movies were made in the Northeast. But moviemakers needed sunny days to film outdoors. The Northeast is often cloudy and rainy. A few moviemakers found the sunshine they needed in Southern California. Others soon followed.

The movie industry soon attracted a man named Walt Disney. Disney arrived in Southern California in 1923 with one big goal. He wanted to make people happy. And he did. Disney's cartoons delighted kids of all ages. So did his movies, television shows, and the "magic kingdom" of Disneyland.

Disneyland opened in 1955. It was a huge success. This year, as many as 14 million people will visit the park. Do you know why? It still makes people happy!

Disneyland's Sleeping Beauty Castle was designed in the style of European castles from the Middle Ages.

12.6 California's Central Valley: America's Fruit and Salad Bowl

Do you snack on raisins? Spread strawberry jam on your toast? Pour ketchup on your French fries? Look around you. Those foods probably came from California's Central Valley.

The Central Valley is shaped like a long bathtub. The sides are formed by mountain ranges. The bottom is covered with deep, rich soil. Summers here are long and warm.

Does this sound like a good place to farm? It is. But there is a problem. Almost no rain falls during the growing season.

California has solved this problem by building dams on rivers flowing down from the mountains. Water collects behind the dams in winter. In the summer, this water is used to irrigate crops.

technology the use of tools and ideas to meet people's needs

Irrigation turned the Central Valley into America's fruit and salad bowl. More than 150 fruits and vegetables are raised here. You probably eat some of them every day.

The Central Valley is also a center of farming technology. **Technology** is the use of tools and ideas to meet people's needs. Scientists here have invented many machines to help farmers pick their crops. One is a tomato-picking machine. This machine is so gentle that it can pick up an egg and pack it in a box without breaking it.

These California tomatoes are harvested by machine.

12.7 The Columbia River Gorge National Scenic Area

We have reached the Columbia River Gorge National Scenic Area. A **gorge** is a deep, narrow valley with steep walls. The Columbia River cut this beautiful gorge out of rock.

The Columbia River begins in the Rocky Mountains in Canada. It flows 1,200 miles south and west into the Pacific Ocean. For much of its journey, the river forms the boundary between the states of Washington and Oregon.

The Columbia looks lazy here. But don't let that fool you. This is one hardworking river. Dams on the river help make a lot of electricity. Many businesses use this electric power. Farmers use water from the river to irrigate crops. Columbia River waters irrigate more than 8 million acres of land.

Both farmers and businesspeople use the river for transportation. Many goods travel on the Columbia to shipping centers. It is the second most traveled river in the country. Only the Mississippi River carries more goods.

Putting the river to work has been good for people. Both Oregon and Washington are growing rapidly. But it has been bad for fish—especially salmon.

Since 1850, the number of salmon in the Columbia River has dropped sharply. Do you know why? You'll find out during our stop at the gorge.

Washington lies to the north of the Columbia River Gorge. Oregon lies to the south.

gorge a deep, narrow valley

Salmon Returning to the Columbia River

Millions of Salmon

Year

Dam built

Dam built

12.8 A Sawmill in Tacoma, Washington

Welcome to Tacoma, Washington. Tacoma was founded 150 years ago as a logging town. Today, Tacoma is still a center of the wood products industry. Wood products include lumber, plywood, cardboard, and paper.

We are visiting a **sawmill** in Tacoma. There are two things I like about touring a sawmill. The first is seeing giant saws turn logs into lumber. The second is the smell of freshly sawn wood.

What I don't like is the noise. Every time a saw cuts into a log, it makes a screaming sound. When that happens, you may want to cover your ears.

Can you guess how much wood this country uses each year? Imagine building a walkway 30 feet wide with all the wood Americans use in a year. How far do you think it would reach? All the way to the moon! That's a lot of wood.

Much of that wood comes from the West. In the 1800s, forests attracted loggers and lumbermen to this region. The mountains of the West were covered with forests. Today many westerners still work in the lumber industry.

We are heading now for Seattle-Tacoma International Airport. We'll take a plane to our next stop. Be sure to fasten your seat belts for takeoff.

sawmill a factory where logs are turned into lumber

These stacks of sawn lumber will eventually be shipped to customers around the world.

12.9 Anchorage, Alaska: Starting Point of the Iditarod

We are in Anchorage, Alaska. Alaska is by far the largest of the United States. And yet it has the fewest number of people of any state. Can you guess why? One reason is its chilly climate.

Alaska is farther from the equator than any other state. As a result, it is the coldest state. Its winters are so cold that houseflies can't survive here.

People have been attracted to Alaska by its resources. In 1899, gold was discovered near the town of Nome. In no time, Nome grew from 300 to more than 30,000 people. Another rush of people began in 1968. That year, oil was discovered in northern Alaska.

Today many people come to Alaska to enjoy its open spaces and outdoor activities. A favorite sport here is dogsled racing. Alaskans used to depend on dogsleds to get around in winter. Now they use airplanes and snowmobiles.

The most famous dogsled race is the Iditarod. The Iditarod begins right here in Anchorage. It ends 1,150 miles later in Nome. A few teams of dogs and their mushers, or drivers, have covered that distance in an amazing nine days. No wonder Alaskans call this event the "Last Great Race on Earth."

Iditarod teams typically have 16 or 18 dogs, which pull the sled at an average speed of about 10 miles per hour.

If you get tired of the crowds at Waikiki Beach, you can hike 760 feet up Diamond Head to see the crater that was formed by a violent explosion of steam.

12.10 Honolulu, Hawaii: A Tourist Paradise

You have just flown from our country's coldest state to its warmest. Hawaii lies closer to the equator than any other U.S. state. Its climate is sunny and warm all year round.

We are looking at Waikiki Beach in Honolulu, Hawaii. I grew up near here. My father gave me my first surfing lesson at Waikiki. Maybe I'll have a chance to teach you how to surf here.

Today, tourists from all over the world enjoy this sunny beach. Tourism is Hawaii's most important industry. But it wasn't always such a big deal.

A hundred years ago, the main industry on the Hawaiian Islands was raising sugar cane. Hawaii's sugar planters needed lots of workers for their plantations. Those workers came from China, Japan, the Philippines, Portugal, and other places.

My great-great-grandparents came to Hawaii from Japan around 1890. They planned to work in the sugar fields a few years, and then return home. But they liked Hawaii and decided to stay.

My grandfather remembers when jet airplanes began flying to Hawaii. That was in the 1950s. Airplanes made it easier for tourists to come to Hawaii. Today many jobs in Hawaii are related to tourism. So, we are very happy you are visiting our islands.

12.11 Chapter Summary

What an awesome tour! We began high in the Rocky Mountains and ended up on Waikiki Beach. Along the way, we saw sights in eight states.

What was your favorite stop? The mine entrance in Leadville? Disneyland? The Columbia River? Can you guess mine? It's Waikiki Beach, of course.

Remember the two questions I asked when we began our tour? What first attracted people to the West? And why are people still coming here today?

Here are my answers to the first question. People first came to the West in search of adventure, opportunity, and sunshine. The West had beautiful places to explore. It had valuable natural resources. These resources included furs, gold, silver, oil, and forests. And it had a climate that attracted moviemakers and farmers.

My answers to the second question are the same. People still come to the West for adventure, opportunity, and sunshine. The adventures have changed. We now hike and ski in the region where Lewis and Clark once almost starved.

The opportunities have changed. Today there are more jobs in the tourism and entertainment industries than in mining or logging.

But the sunshine is the same. I hope you had fun in the sun on our trip.

Aloha!

The Golden Gate Bridge spans the entrance to San Francisco Bay.

chapter 13

Cities of the West

13.1 Introduction

"Go west, young man, and grow up with the country!" In the 1850s, these words were heard all over America. Men and women of all ages have been following that advice ever since.

Americans have always viewed the West as a place where they could start new lives. In the 1800s, the West's wide-open spaces attracted farmers, miners, and ranchers. Today, the West still has mines, ranches, and lots of land. It also has lively cities that attract people from around the world.

In this chapter, you will learn about seven of these cities. In each city, you'll visit an interesting place that tells something important about the city. As you read the chapter, ask yourself this question: "What is attracting people to the West today?"

Television Commercial Promoting the West

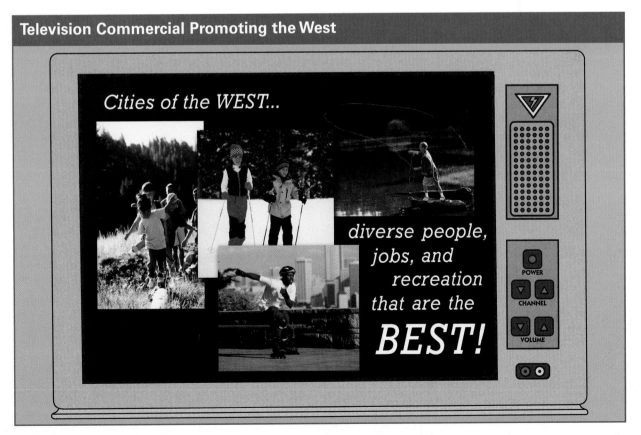

Cities of the WEST...

diverse people, jobs, and recreation that are the BEST!

Denver, the capital of Colorado, is one of the nation's fastest-growing cities.

mint a factory where coins are made

13.2 Denver, Colorado

Denver, Colorado, is home to the U.S. Mint. A **mint** is where coins—such as dimes, nickels, quarters, and pennies—are made. Back in the 1860s, miners brought their gold here. Their nuggets were melted and turned into valuable gold bars. The mint began producing gold and silver coins in 1906. Today, the mint makes about 50 million coins every day!

Geography and Climate

Denver is located where the Great Plains meet the Rocky Mountains. Denver is known as the "Mile High City." If you stand on the 18th step of the state capitol building, you'll be exactly 5,280 feet, or one mile, above sea level. By the way, the dome of the capitol building is covered with real Colorado gold!

Denver has a dry, sunny climate. The city gets snow in the winter. (See the chart on page 167.)

History

Denver was founded in 1858 after gold was discovered in the area. Smaller mining communities grew up around the city.

During World War II, many U.S. government offices moved to Denver. After the war, many people decided to stay there.

Population

In 2000, a little more than half a million people lived in the city of Denver. The city's population is becoming very diverse. According to the 2000 census, about half of Denver's residents are white. Almost a third (30 percent) are Latino, and about 10 percent are African American.

Economy

Most people in Denver work for the U.S. government. In fact, Denver has more government workers than Washington, D.C. Many large companies are also located in Denver.

Fun Things to Do

Denver offers lots of opportunities for having fun. The city has more than 250 parks with trails for cycling, running, and walking. Denver even has a park where a herd of buffalo lives.

Denver is the center of professional sports in the Rocky Mountain region. The city's major league teams include the Denver Broncos (football), the Colorado Rockies (baseball), the Denver Nuggets (basketball), and the Colorado Avalanche (ice hockey). Every January, Denver is the site of a national cattle show and rodeo.

Rodeo fans watch cowboys and cowgirls compete in such events as bronco riding, calf roping, and steer wrestling.

The capital of Utah, Salt Lake City is named for the huge saltwater lake that lies west of the city.

Mormons members of the Church of Jesus Christ of Latter-day Saints

13.3 Salt Lake City, Utah

If you stand in the center of downtown Salt Lake City, Utah, you will be in Temple Square. In front of you will be a huge white building, the Mormon Temple. Temple Square has always been the heart of Salt Lake City. The city was started by a group of people called **Mormons**. The Mormons built the city around their temple. The temple itself took 40 years to build!

Geography and Climate

Salt Lake City is in the north-central part of Utah. It is located in a high valley between the Wasatch Mountains and the Great Salt Lake Desert.

The climate in Salt Lake City is dry. The city has warm summers, and some snow in the winter. (See the chart on page 167.)

History

Salt Lake City was settled in 1847 by members of the Church of Jesus Christ of Latter-day Saints, also known as Mormons. The Mormons were looking for a place where they could freely practice their religion. When they first arrived at the site of Salt Lake City, it was a desertlike area. The Mormons used irrigation to bring water to the dry valley. They turned a desert into farmland.

In the 1880s, Salt Lake City's population more than doubled because of nearby mining. The city grew again during World War II. The government needed metal for ships and planes, so more people came to work in the mines. Many wartime workers stayed and settled in the Salt Lake City area.

Population

In 2000, over 180,000 people lived in Salt Lake City. If you include the nearby towns, more than 1 million people live in the area.

Salt Lake City's population was once almost entirely white. But it has become more diverse over the years. In 2000, whites made up about 70 percent of the city's population. Latinos were the second largest group (almost 19 percent). Asians and Pacific Islanders were the third largest group (5.5 percent).

People of all ages enjoy cross-country skiing around the Wasatch Mountains.

Economy

Mining is one of the city's most important industries. Copper, silver, lead, zinc, coal, and iron ore are all mined nearby.

Fun Things to Do

The Wasatch Mountains tower over the city. They are a wonderful place for hiking and skiing. Because of this, Salt Lake City was chosen as the site of the 2002 Winter Olympics. The city also has many parks.

Salt Lake City has one major league sports team, the Utah Jazz (basketball).

13.4 Boise, Idaho

A fun time to visit Boise, Idaho, is during its River Festival in June. Every year, this summer party goes on for four days. It features classic car shows, concerts, fireworks, parades, and other events.

One of the biggest treats at the festival is seeing the sky filled with hot-air balloons. Early each morning, the balloons rise from a park. The colorful balloons come in all kinds of shapes—even dinosaurs, cows, and rabbits!

Geography and Climate

Boise is located on the Boise River in southwestern Idaho. It is near the Salmon River Mountains. Boise has a dry, sunny climate, with some snow in the winter. (See the chart on page 167.)

History

Boise was started in 1863, after gold was discovered in the region. The U.S. government built a fort near the Boise River. The city was built next to the fort.

Boise grew rapidly as miners rushed to the goldfields. Many of the miners were immigrants from China. In 1925, the Union Pacific Railroad ran its main line through Boise. This made even more people want to live in this city. Boise continued to grow in the 1980s, when new electronics factories created more jobs.

The state capitol building in Boise, Idaho, uses hot water pumped from under the ground for heat.

Population

Between 1990 and 2000, Boise's population grew from about 125,000 people to more than 185,000. If you count nearby towns, more than 400,000 people live in the Boise area.

In 2000, about 90 percent of Boise's people were white. The next largest groups were Latinos (4.5 percent) and Asians and Pacific Islanders (2.3 percent).

Economy

Boise provides banking, shopping, and health services for many people. Lots of people work for companies that make forest products and computer chips.

Fun Things to Do

People in Boise enjoy the outdoors. There are lots of pathways for walking, bicycling, skating, and jogging. In a set of parks called the Greenbelt, people have picnics, play sports, watch birds, and listen to concerts. Places to ski and go whitewater rafting are within an easy drive of the city.

The Boise River Festival attracts thousands of visitors every year. Sports fans in Boise can root for the city's minor league baseball and ice hockey teams.

Fly-fishing is a popular sport in and around Boise.

Seattle is Washington's largest city. A fleet of ferryboats helps connect Seattle to other parts of the state and to Canada.

13.5 Seattle, Washington

The best place to see Seattle, Washington, is from the top of the city's most famous landmark, the Space Needle. An elevator lifts you 52 stories above the ground. From there, you can look out at Seattle's skyscrapers and the ferryboats crossing Elliott Bay.

The Space Needle was built for the 1962 World's Fair. It still looks like something out of the future. That makes it a perfect landmark for this modern city.

Geography and Climate

Seattle is in the northwestern corner of the United States, about 100 miles south of the border with Canada. The city lies next to a large bay of the Pacific Ocean. It is surrounded by mountains.

Seattle has a mild, rainy climate. The city is often cloudy or foggy. (See the chart on page 167.)

History

Seattle was started in 1851 by a small group of settlers. It grew rapidly in the late nineteenth century with the timber industry and the discovery of gold. Miners poured into Seattle on their way to the goldfields. When the gold rush was over, many of them settled in the city.

Population

The 2000 census counted over half a million people living in Seattle. More than 3 million people live in the surrounding area. This is one of the fastest-growing regions in the United States.

In 2000, whites made up about 68 percent of Seattle's population. The next largest group was Asians and Pacific Islanders (more than 13 percent).

Economy

Seattle is an important port in the United States. Here, goods are traded with Japan and Asia. Fishing and lumber are also important resources in Seattle.

For many years, most jobs in Seattle were at a company that made airplanes. Now, many people have jobs in the computer industry.

Fun Things to Do

Seattle has more than 5,000 acres of public land. People enjoy miles of trails where they can cycle, skate, jog, and walk. The nearby mountains offer excellent skiing, climbing, and hiking. The area's many lakes make boating and fishing popular pastimes.

Seattle has three major league sports teams: the Mariners (baseball), the Seahawks (football), and the Supersonics (basketball).

Miles and miles of paved trails make Seattle a great city for outdoor activities.

13.6 Portland, Oregon

In spring, roses bloom in gardens all over the city of Portland, Oregon. In fact, one of Portland's biggest attractions is the International Rose Test Garden. Here you can see 10,000 rosebushes and more than 500 varieties of roses in all colors. Some people call Portland the "City of Roses."

Geography and Climate

Portland is located on the banks of the Willamette River in northwestern Oregon. The city lies in a fertile valley between the Coast and Cascade Mountain Ranges.

Portland's climate is mild, with heavy rains in the late fall and winter. (See the chart on page 167.)

History

Portland got its start in 1845. Settlers arrived by the thousands over the Oregon Trail. During the California gold rush, Portland grew rapidly. Settlers sold lumber and grain to miners and their families in California.

The Willamette River winds through Portland, Oregon.

Portland continued to grow at a steady pace. In 1905, a world's fair brought 3 million visitors to the city. Many of them decided to stay. In the 1930s, dams on the Columbia and Willamette Rivers provided cheap electricity. This brought a number of industries to Portland. During World War II, thousands of workers arrived in the city to build ships.

Population

In 2000, Portland's population was more than half a million people. Close to 2 million people live in the city and its surrounding areas.

According to the 2000 census, more than three fourths of Portland's residents are white. Most of the rest of the population is divided equally among Latinos, African Americans, and Asians and Pacific Islanders.

Economy

People in Portland work for various kinds of companies. Some make paper. Others make clothing and shoes. Portland also has new businesses, such as computer software companies.

Portland's harbor is one of the busiest in the country. Shipping companies have been there for many years.

Fun Things to Do

Portland is well known for its parks and open spaces. Forest Park, which covers nearly 5,000 acres, is one of the largest natural areas inside a U.S. city. Less than 50 miles away, Mount Hood is a great place for skiing and other winter sports. The annual Rose Festival in June draws visitors from throughout the Pacific Northwest.

Portland has one major league sports team, the Portland Trail Blazers (basketball).

Walking and hiking clubs are popular in Portland.

The largest city in Northern California, San Jose has well over 2,000 miles of streets.

13.7 San Jose, California

San Jose, California, calls itself the "Capital of Silicon Valley." Silicon Valley is a nickname for the area between the cities of San Jose and San Francisco. Silicon is a material used to make the brains of a computer. The first computer companies began in Silicon Valley in the 1970s.

Geography and Climate

San Jose is located near the southern tip of San Francisco Bay. The city has a mild to warm climate. (See the chart on page 167.)

History

Spanish settlers founded San Jose in 1777. For many years, the area was home to vineyards and orchards. The city changed greatly after World War II, when new businesses were built. By 1980, the city had spread out to almost 10 times its size in 1950.

Population

San Jose's population had reached nearly 900,000 people by the year 2000. The city's population is very diverse. Only about 36 percent of the people are white. Nearly as many are Latino (30 percent), and more than 26 percent are Asians or Pacific Islanders.

Economy

The San Jose region is famous for its technology companies. Silicon Valley is home to some of the best-known high-technology companies in the world. San Jose also has several large factories that process canned foods.

Fun Things to Do

San Jose has about 75 parks and playgrounds. The largest park is Alum Rock Park. It has miles of trails for hiking and horseback riding. Fans of thrill rides can go to amusement parks in nearby Santa Clara and Santa Cruz.

San Jose has two major league sports teams, the Sharks (ice hockey) and the Earthquakes (soccer).

Many people in San Jose work in the technology field. This woman is testing parts for computers.

Las Vegas comes alive at night. It is the largest city in Nevada.

13.8 Las Vegas, Nevada

As you drive into Las Vegas, Nevada, you will see a sign that reads, "Welcome to Fabulous Las Vegas." And *fabulous* is certainly the word for this city of bright lights and hotels. Everywhere you look, colorful signs advertise music, comedy, and magic shows. It's no wonder Las Vegas calls itself the "Entertainment Capital of the World"!

Geography and Climate

Las Vegas is near the southern tip of Nevada. It is in a desert valley that is surrounded by mountains.

Las Vegas has a dry climate. Winters are warm, and summers are hot. (See chart on page 167.)

History

Las Vegas lies in one of the few places in the desert that has water and trees. Such a place is called an **oasis**. Spanish explorers discovered this oasis in the late 1820s. Las Vegas remained a small town until the 1930s. Then, construction began on the Hoover Dam. The dam project created thousands of new jobs. Many of the workers stayed to settle in Las Vegas.

After World War II, Las Vegas grew rapidly as more and more hotels and casinos were built. Today, about 30 million visitors come to play in Las Vegas every year.

oasis a place in the desert that has water and trees

Population

In 2000, about half a million people lived in Las Vegas. Almost 60 percent of the city's people were white. The next largest groups were Latinos (about 24 percent) and African Americans (about 10 percent).

Economy

Tourism is a big business in Las Vegas. The city's restaurants, hotels, and shops provide thousands of jobs. There is also great demand for home building and landscaping.

Fun Things to Do

Las Vegas is famous for its shows. Many world-famous singers, dancers, and comics have performed there. Championship boxing matches are often held in Las Vegas.

People in Las Vegas also have fun at outdoor activities. They can hike and camp. They can fish and boat on nearby lakes. And the Grand Canyon is only a five-hour car drive away.

The building of new hotels and other structures in Las Vegas creates many construction jobs.

City High Temperatures and Populations

CITY	AVG. JANUARY HIGH	AVG. JULY HIGH	POPULATION
Denver	43.2°F	88.2°F	554,636
Salt Lake City	36.4°F	92.8°F	181,743
Boise	36.4°F	90.2°F	185,787
Seattle	46.3°F	74.4°F	563,374
Portland	45.4°F	79.7°F	529,121
San Jose	57.8°F	74.2°F	894,943
Las Vegas	57.5°F	103.5°F	478,434

Temperature data from the National Oceanic and Atmospheric Administration, based on averages for the years 1961–1990. Population data from the U.S. Census Bureau.

13.9 Chapter Summary

Pioneers loaded up their belongings in covered wagons. They traveled to the West to start new lives. Today, the West is still a magnet for people from all around the world. Of course, they don't drive covered wagons, and few will start a farm or a ranch. Instead, they are settling down in one of the West's thriving cities.

Have you discovered what attracts newcomers to the West today? Here are some clues:

- climate
- recreational opportunities
- scenery
- new businesses and industries
- diverse populations

The growth of cities also creates problems for people to solve. In many western cities, people worry about traffic, crowding, and the cost of homes. They are concerned about clean air and water. They want to keep all the good things that first attracted them to the West. Would solving these problems make people of the West modern pioneers?

Researching Your State's Geography

14.1 Introduction

Imagine that you are flying in an airplane over your state. When you look down, do you see mountains or flat plains? A desert or a sandy coast? Are there lots of trees, lakes, and rivers? Is it cloudy and raining? Or is the sun shining brightly on your state?

These features of land, water, and sky are part of your state's geography. Studying the geography of a place is important. It helps explain how and why people live in a place. People must often adapt, or change, how they live to fit their environment.

From your airplane, you can also see cities and towns, roads and highways, bridges and dams. Geography includes the study of these constructed features as well. They show how people have altered, or changed, their environment to make their lives more comfortable.

Imagine now that you are a geographer. What can you find out about the geography of your state?

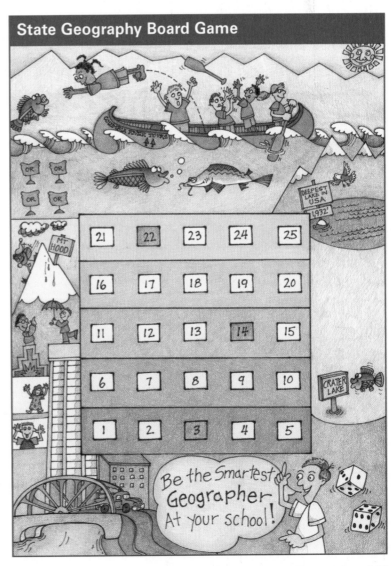

State Geography Board Game

14.2 What Tools Do Geographers Use?

Geographers use many tools to learn about different places and the people who live there. Some of these tools are maps, charts, and graphs. They help organize facts and information.

In Chapter 2, you learned about three kinds of maps. You might use these types of maps to help you discover facts about your state's geography. What could you learn about your state from a physical map or a political map? What could you discover from a specialty map of the growing seasons in your state?

You can also get interesting facts from charts and graphs. A chart might give information about the industries in your state. These facts might give you clues about the natural resources in your area. Or you might find a graph showing the average monthly temperatures and rainfall in your state. What could these facts tell you about how people work and play in your state?

The study of facts about the people in an area is called *demographics*. Such facts might include the average age of people in a state. They might compare the number of men to the number of women living in a state. This information often appears on charts and graphs, too.

This map of Florida offers information about the state's size, shape, and location.

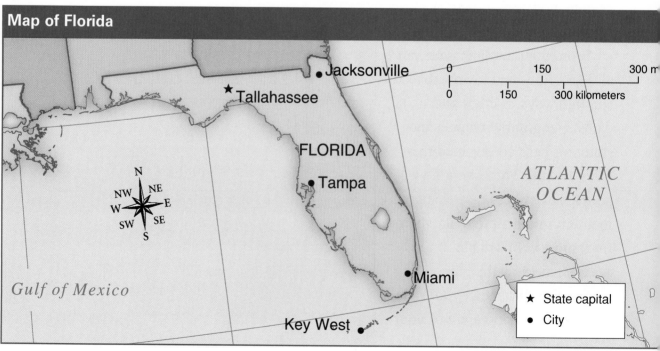

Map of Florida

14.3 Finding Out About the Geography of Your State

There are lots of ways to research the geography of your state. Try these sources of information:

Atlases and encyclopedias. An atlas is a book of maps. An encyclopedia contains facts about all kinds of topics. Find a map of your state in an atlas. Then look up your state in an encyclopedia.

The Internet. The Internet is a fast way to find information. First, connect to the Internet on a computer. Then, type the name of your state plus a word such as *geography* or *climate*. Read the list of Web sites that appear on the screen. Click on any that sound interesting.

Libraries. Start your research in the reference section of the library. Look for books, newspaper and magazine articles, journals, and diaries about your state. Maps, drawings, and photographs might be interesting, too. Ask a librarian for help.

Chambers of commerce. Most cities and towns have an office called the chamber of commerce. Visit yours to find brochures, maps, postcards, and books about your state's geography and attractions.

State departments of tourism. Try writing to your state's department of tourism for information. Or visit your state's department of tourism Web site on the Internet.

The Internet has become an important tool for people interested in learning more about geography.

chapter 15

Researching Your State's History

15.1 Introduction

What is your state like? How did it get to be that way? Who settled your state? Who built its towns, cities, and farms? Why did these people choose your state as a place to live?

Questions like these are what history is all about. Studying history is like solving a mystery. When you study history, you use all kinds of clues to figure out what went on in the past.

These clues can be written records, like journals, newspapers, and letters. They can also be things you see around you, like old buildings. Each of these clues has a story to tell about the past.

Finding out about your state's history can help you appreciate the place where you live. It can help you understand why your state is the way it is today. It can even help you figure out what your state might be like in the future.

Historical Building

15.2 The Settlement of a State

The first people to live in your state were Native Americans. These people probably came to your state looking for a good place to hunt or to grow food.

About 500 years ago, Europeans began to arrive in North America. Some of these people hoped to find gold and other riches. Some came to trap animals for their furs. Many came in search of a place where they would have the freedom to live the way they wanted.

Since then, people have continued to come to America from all around the world. Like the earlier settlers, these newer arrivals have been looking for a better life.

For many people, a better life means a chance for a good job. For others, it means living in a place with a good climate for growing crops. Some people like the excitement of big cities. Others like wide-open spaces.

What can you find out about why people chose your state as a place to live? What opportunities has your state given people for a better life? How have these opportunities changed over time?

Before railroads criss-crossed the country, some pioneers traveled west in Conestoga wagons. These wagons were ideal for carrying heavy loads and traveling along rocky trails.

15.3 The Growth and Development of a State

Comparing the states in our country is like comparing people. They are alike in many ways, and different in others. Each is special in its own way.

In some states, towns and cities crowd together. Other states have miles and miles of open spaces. Some states have lots of businesses and factories. Other are mostly farmland.

States developed in different ways because of their natural resources. Midwestern states like Iowa offered settlers rich soil for farming. In Colorado, miners found gold and silver. In Texas, ranchers found grasslands that were perfect for raising cattle.

States also differ because of the people who settled them. The colony of Pennsylvania welcomed people of all religions. People from many countries settled in this state. Its population is still very diverse today. In California, French and Italian settlers brought their grape-growing talents to their new home. They planted vineyards that today produce world-famous grapes.

Each state has its own story. What can you find out about how your state has grown and developed?

The discovery of gold in Alaska in the late 1890s brought thousands of miners through the state of Washington. The city of Seattle grew as people found work providing the miners with clothing and transportation.

chapter 16

Researching Your State's Economy

16.1 Introduction

What kind of job would you like to have someday? Would you like to work with people as a teacher, a salesperson, or a lawyer? Would you like to design clothes or create computer programs? Would you like to work with your hands as a carpenter or a mechanic?

Thousands of jobs like these are part of your state's economy. An economy is made up of all the ways that people make and sell goods and services.

Goods are objects you can buy, such as food, clothing, and cars. Services are things that we pay others to do for us. Restaurants save people the trouble of cooking. Travel agents help people plan their next vacation or business trip.

Studying your state's economy helps you understand how people live and work in your state. It can also help you learn what kinds of jobs might be waiting for you in the future.

Types of Jobs

16.2 A State's Economy Grows and Develops

Each state's economy grows and develops in different ways. A state's natural resources and climate often determine the goods a state makes and sells. These factors also influence who visits and lives in a state. A state's economy is dependent on its people. As people's needs change, so does a state's economy.

The state of Florida is a good example. Florida's first big industry was agriculture, or farming. Florida's rich soil and warm, wet climate made it a perfect place to grow sugar cane and citrus fruits, such as oranges. Then tourists began coming to Florida to enjoy its sunny weather and natural features. As a result, tourism became a huge industry, creating jobs in hotels, restaurants, shops, and amusement parks. Florida's pleasant climate also attracted millions of retired people. Stores and many kinds of services developed to take care of the needs of these people.

Montana's economy was also based on its climate and natural resources. In addition to agriculture, Montana developed lumbering, mining, and ranching industries. As the state's population grew and changed, so did its economy. Today, more people in Montana work in services and in stores than in any other type of business.

The state of Washington has ideal conditions for growing cranberries.

16.3 Types of Industry in the United States

Many types of industries and jobs, or economic activities, are found in almost every state. Here are some that you can find in your state. Can you think of others?

Agriculture. The agriculture industry is made up of any business that produces food. Farmworkers, fishermen, and ranchers work in agriculture. Scientists and businesspeople also work in this industry.

Manufacturing. Any business that makes things for people to buy is part of the manufacturing industry. Factory workers, scientists, and engineers are just a few of the people who work in manufacturing.

Retail. Stores that sell things to the public make up the retail industry. Supermarkets, video stores, and car dealerships are all retail businesses. Two of the main jobs in retail are sales clerks and store managers.

Government. Millions of people work for federal, state, and local governments. Governments need many kinds of workers. Teachers, firefighters, and police officers work for governments.

Service. Many people work in service businesses. Hairdressers, dry cleaners, auto repair workers, and security guards all provide services to the public.

The service industry is made up of many types of jobs. This airport ground crewman is part of the service industry.

chapter 17

Researching Your State's Government

17.1 Introduction

Do you see things that you would like to change in your state? Perhaps you'd like to see schools get more money to fix their buildings. Maybe you'd like to see somebody take better care of your state parks. Or maybe you'd like to see stronger laws against dangerous drivers.

There are always new problems to worry about as things change around us. In the United States, the **federal government** is concerned with problems that affect the whole country. State governments worry about problems that affect their state.

To solve problems, governments make new laws. The federal government makes laws for the entire United States. Your state government makes laws for your state. It also makes sure people obey these laws.

As a **citizen,** you can have a big effect on what your state government does. But first you need to know how your state government works.

Places of Government

17.2 How State Governments Work

Do you know the capital city of your state? That is where you will find the main offices of your state government.

State governments work the same way as the federal government. They are divided into three parts, called *branches*.

The **legislative branch** writes the laws. In the federal government, Congress writes laws. In each state, a group called the *state legislature* writes laws.

The U.S. Congress contains two parts, called *houses*. One house is the Senate, and the other is the House of Representatives. Most states also have two houses. They call these houses the *state senate* and the *state assembly*.

The **executive branch** enforces the laws. In the federal government, the president is in charge of the executive branch. In each state, the governor is the head of the executive branch.

The **judicial branch** settles disagreements about the laws. In the federal government, this branch includes the Supreme Court and other federal courts. In the states, the judicial branch is made up of state courts and judges.

legislative branch the part of government that writes laws

executive branch the part of government that enforces laws

judicial branch the part of government that settles disagreements about laws

The State Legislature

The Governor

The State Courts

17.3 How Ideas Become Laws

Suppose you have an idea for a new state law. How could you make your law a reality?

The first step is to get other people's support. When many citizens get behind an idea, state governments will listen to them. That's because citizens elect their governors and state legislators.

There are many ways to get people's support. For example, you could hang posters around town. You could write letters to the newspaper. You could go to town meetings. You could call up television or radio talk shows. You could organize rallies.

For an idea to become law, a stage legislator must write a **bill**. The legislature debates the bill and often makes changes to it. Then the legislature votes on the bill.

If the legislature approves the bill, the governor must agree to sign it. Otherwise, the bill does not become law.

Sometimes people believe that a state law is unfair. When that happens, they might ask state courts to take a look at the law. Courts can overrule a law when it disagrees with the U.S. Constitution or with the state **constitution**.

This member of Congress is talking to a group of students on Capitol Hill.

bill a proposal for a new law
constitution a written statement of a plan for government

183

The Pledge of Allegiance

I pledge allegiance to the flag
of the United States of America,
and to the Republic
for which it stands,
one Nation under God, indivisible,
with liberty and justice for all.

The Star-Spangled Banner

September 20, 1814
By Francis Scott Key

O, say, can you see, by the dawn's early light,
What so proudly we hailed at the twilight's last gleaming?
Whose broad stripes and bright stars, through the perilous fight,
O'er the ramparts we watched, were so gallantly streaming?
And the rockets' red glare, the bombs bursting in air,
Gave proof through the night that our flag was still there.
O say, does that star-spangled banner yet wave
O'er the land of the free and the home of the brave?

On the shore, dimly seen through the mists of the deep,
Where the foe's haughty host in dread silence reposes,
What is that which the breeze, o'er the towering steep,
As it fitfully blows, now conceals, now discloses?
Now it catches the gleam of the morning's first beam,
In full glory reflected now shines on the stream:
'Tis the star-spangled banner! O long may it wave
O'er the land of the free and the home of the brave.

And where is that band who so vauntingly swore
That the havoc of war and the battle's confusion
A home and a country should leave us no more?
Their blood has wiped out their foul footstep's pollution.
No refuge could save the hireling and slave
From the terror of flight, or the gloom of the grave:
And the star-spangled banner in triumph doth wave
O'er the land of the free and the home of the brave.

Oh! thus be it ever, when freemen shall stand
Between their loved homes and the war's desolation!
Blest with victory and peace, may the heaven-rescued land
Praise the Power that hath made and preserved us a nation.
Then conquer we must, for our cause it is just,
And this be our motto: "In God is our trust."
And the star-spangled banner forever shall wave
O'er the land of the free and the home of the brave!

0°   40°   80°   120°   160°

ARCTIC OCEAN   SEVERNAYA ZEMLYA   ARCTIC OCEAN   80°
SVALBARD
ZEMLYA FRANTSA IOSIFA

Novaya Zemlya

Area of Inset

Arctic Circle

EUROPE

RUSSIA

ASIA

KAZAKHSTAN

MONGOLIA   ALEUTIAN ISLANDS   40°

GEORGIA   UZBEKISTAN   KYRGYZSTAN   NORTH
ARMENIA   AZERBAIJAN   KOREA
TURKMENISTAN   TAJIKISTAN   CHINA   SOUTH   JAPAN
CYPRUS   SYRIA   KOREA
MOROCCO   TUNISIA   LEBANON   IRAQ   AFGHANISTAN
ISRAEL   IRAN
RY   ALGERIA   JORDAN   PAKISTAN   NEPAL   BHUTAN
DS   LIBYA   EGYPT   SAUDI   QATAR   BANGLADESH   TAIWAN   Tropic of Cancer
TERN   ARABIA   U.A.E.   BURMA
HARA   AFRICA   INDIA   LAOS   PACIFIC
URITANIA   ERITREA   OMAN   THAILAND   VIETNAM   OCEAN
AL   MALI   NIGER   CHAD   YEMEN   CAMBODIA   PHILIPPINES
BURKINA   SUDAN   DJIBOUTI
GUINEA   FASO   NIGERIA   ETHIOPIA   SRI   BRUNEI
IERRA   IVORY   CENTRAL   LANKA   MALAYSIA
EONE   COAST   AFRICAN REPUBLIC   SOMALIA
LIBERIA   CAMEROON   UGANDA   EAST INDIES   0°
GHANA   CONGO   KENYA   MELANESIA
INEA-BISSAU   GABON   RWANDA   SINGAPORE   INDONESIA   PAPUA
MBIA   REPUBLIC   BURUNDI   NEW   SOLOMON
TOGO   OF CONGO   TANZANIA   GUINEA   ISLANDS
BENIN
EQUATORIAL   INDIAN
GUINEA   ANGOLA   MALAWI   OCEAN   Coral Sea   VANUATU   FIJI
ZAMBIA   MOZAMBIQUE   MAURITIUS
SOUTH   NAMIBIA   ZIMBABWE   MADAGASCAR
TLANTIC   BOTSWANA   RÉUNION   AUSTRALIA   Tropic of Capricorn
OCEAN   AUSTRALIA
SWAZILAND
SOUTH   LESOTHO
AFRICA
North I.   NEW
ZEALAND   40°
South I.

N
W   E
S

0   2000   4000 miles (at equator)

0   2000   4000   6000 kilometers (at equator)

Gall projection

Antarctic Circle

ANTARCTICA

0°   40°   80°   120°   160°

World Physical Map

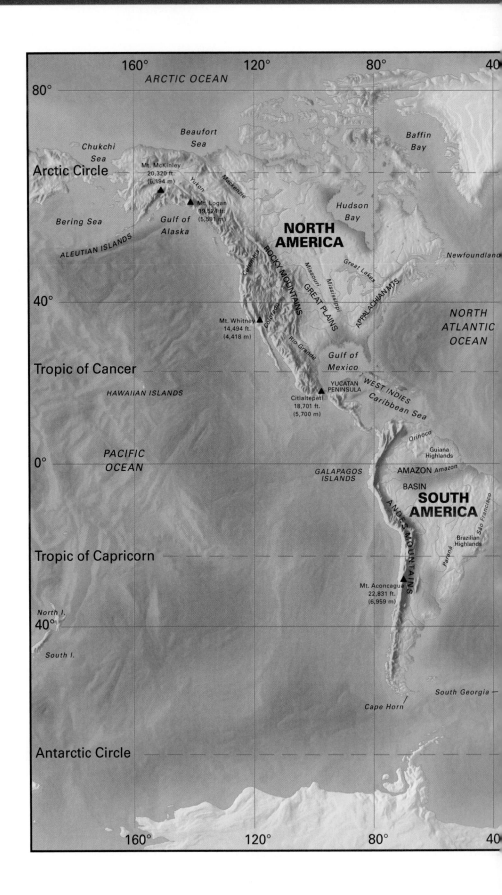

ARCTIC OCEAN

160°   120°   80°   40°

80°

Chukchi
Sea

Beaufort
Sea

Baffin
Bay

Arctic Circle

Mt. McKinley
20,320 ft.
(6,194 m)

Yukon

Mackenzie

Hudson
Bay

Bering Sea

Gulf of
Alaska

Mt. Logan
19,524 ft.
(5,591 m)

**NORTH
AMERICA**

ALEUTIAN ISLANDS

Great Lakes

Newfoundland

Coast Ranges

ROCKY MOUNTAINS

Missouri

Mississippi

40°

Mt. Whitney
14,494 ft.
(4,418 m)

Colorado

GREAT PLAINS

APPALACHIAN MTS.

**NORTH
ATLANTIC
OCEAN**

Tropic of Cancer

Rio Grande

Gulf of
Mexico

HAWAIIAN ISLANDS

YUCATAN
PENINSULA

WEST INDIES

Citlaltepetl
18,701 ft.
(5,700 m)

Caribbean Sea

Orinoco

Guiana
Highlands

0°

PACIFIC
OCEAN

GALAPAGOS
ISLANDS

AMAZON Amazon

BASIN

São Francisco

**SOUTH
AMERICA**

ANDES MOUNTAINS

Brazilian
Highlands

Tropic of Capricorn

Paraná

Mt. Aconcagua
22,831 ft.
(6,959 m)

North I.

40°

South I.

South Georgia

Cape Horn

Antarctic Circle

160°   120°   80°   40°

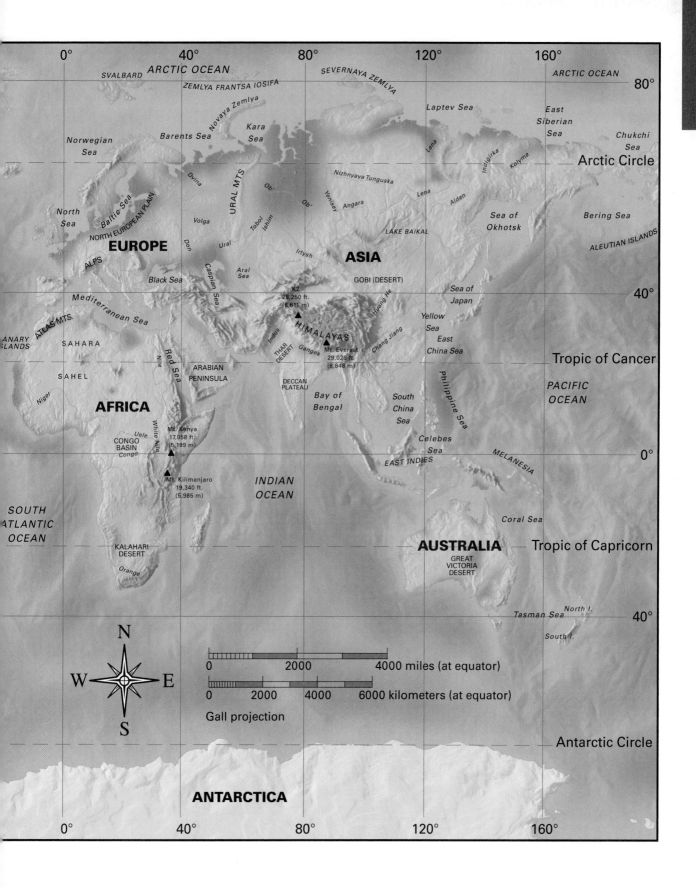

0°   40°   80°   120°   160°

SVALBARD   ARCTIC OCEAN   SEVERNAYA ZEMLYA   ARCTIC OCEAN

80°

ZEMLYA FRANTSA IOSIFA

Novaya Zemlya   Laptev Sea   East Siberian Sea   Chukchi Sea

Norwegian Sea   Barents Sea   Kara Sea

Arctic Circle

Dvina   URAL MTS.   Ob   Nizhnyaya Tunguska   Lena   Indigirka   Kolyma

North Sea   Baltic Sea   Volga   Ob   Yenisey   Angara   Lena   Aldan   Bering Sea

NORTH EUROPEAN PLAIN   Toboi   Ishim   LAKE BAIKAL   Sea of Okhotsk   ALEUTIAN ISLANDS

EUROPE   Don   Ural   Irtysh   ASIA

ALPS   Aral Sea

Black Sea   Caspian Sea   GOBI (DESERT)

Mediterranean Sea   K2 28,250 ft. (8,611 m)   Sea of Japan   40°

ATLAS MTS.   HIMALAYAS   Hwang He   Yellow Sea

CANARY ISLANDS   SAHARA   Indus   THAR DESERT   Ganges   Mt. Everest 29,028 ft. (8,848 m)   Chang Jiang   East China Sea   Tropic of Cancer

SAHEL   Red Sea   ARABIAN PENINSULA   DECCAN PLATEAU   PACIFIC OCEAN

Niger   Nile   Bay of Bengal   South China Sea   Philippine Sea

AFRICA   Uele   White Nile   Mt. Kenya 17,058 ft. (5,199 m)   Celebes Sea   MELANESIA   0°

CONGO BASIN   Congo   EAST INDIES

Mt. Kilimanjaro 19,340 ft. (5,985 m)   INDIAN OCEAN

SOUTH ATLANTIC OCEAN

Coral Sea

KALAHARI DESERT   AUSTRALIA   Tropic of Capricorn

Orange   GREAT VICTORIA DESERT

North I.

Tasman Sea   40°

South I.

N
W   E
S

0   2000   4000 miles (at equator)

0   2000   4000   6000 kilometers (at equator)

Gall projection

Antarctic Circle

ANTARCTICA

0°   40°   80°   120°   160°

CANADA

50°
Lake Winnipegosis
Lake Winnipe[g]
Lake Manitoba
Vancouver Island
C. Flattery
WASHINGTON
Mt. Rainier
Columbia
45°
CASCADE RANGE
ROCKY
Missouri
MONTANA
NORTH DAKOTA
OREGON
IDAHO
Snake
Missouri
MOUNTAINS
WYOMING
Powder
SOUTH DAKOTA
N. Platte
Klamath
40°
C. Mendocino
Great Salt Lake
NEBRAS[KA]
Sacramento
SIERRA NEVADA
NEVADA
UTAH
Colorado
Mt. Elbert
S. Platte
COLORADO
KANS[AS]
Arkansas
Mt. Whitney
35°
CALIFORNIA
Cimarron
Canadian
OKL[AHOMA]
Pt. Arguello
Colorado
ARIZONA
NEW MEXICO
Red
CHANNEL ISLANDS
Gila
Rio Grande
Pecos
GULF OF SANTA CATALINA
30°
TEXA[S]
Rio Grande
130° 125° 120° 115° 110° 105° 100°

Hawaii inset:
22°
Mt. Kawaikini
KAUAI
NIIHAU
Kauai Channel
OAHU
MOLOKAI
21°
LANAI
MAUI
Kolekole
KAHOOLAWE
HAWAII
PACIFIC OCEAN
20°
Mauna Kea
Keahole Point
Mauna Loa
19°
0 50 100 150 miles
0 50 100 150 200 kilometers
Conic projection
160° 159° 158° 157° 156° 155°

Alaska inset:
ARCTIC OCEAN
ARCTIC COASTAL PLAIN
CHUKCHI SEA
Colville
BROOKS RANGE
Kotzebue Sound
Noatak
Kobuk
Koyukuk
Yukon
Bering Strait
Tanana
Norton Sound
ALASKA
St. Lawrence Island
Mt. McKinley
ALASKA
Susitna
Copper
Mt. Bona
Mt. Logan
Nunivak Island
Iliamna Lake
ALEXANDER ARCHIPELAGO
Cape Newenham
GULF OF ALASKA
BRISTOL BAY
Kodiak Island
QUEEN CHARLOTTE ISLANDS
ALASKA
Trinity Islands
Chirikov Island
Unimak Island
Shumagin Islands
0 500 kilometers
0 500 miles
Conical orthomorphic projection
170° 160° 150° 140°
55°
50°

Alabama Alaska Arizona Arkansas

People (2000)

	Alabama	Alaska	Arizona	Arkansas
Population:	4,447,100	626,932	5,130,632	2,637,400
Population Density:	87.6 people per square mile	1.1 people per square mile	45.2 people per square mile	51.3 people per square mile
Racial Distribution:	71.1% white; 26.0% black; 0.5% Native American; 0.7% Asian/Pacific Islander; 1.7% Hispanic	69.3% white; 3.5% black; 15.6% Native American; 4.5% Asian/Pacific Islander; 4.1% Hispanic	75.5% white; 3.1% black; 5.0% Native American; 1.9% Asian/Pacific Islander; 25.3% Hispanic	80.0% white; 15.7% black; 0.8% Native American; 0.9% Asian/Pacific Islander; 3.2% Hispanic

Geography

	Alabama	Alaska	Arizona	Arkansas
Total Area:	52,419 square miles	663,267 square miles	113,998 square miles	53,179 square miles
Climate:	long, hot summers; mild winters; generally abundant rainfall	moist and mild; far N, extremely dry; extended summer days/winter nights	clear and dry in southern regions and northern plateau; heavy winter snows in high central areas	long, hot summers, mild winters; generally abundant rainfall
Topography:	coastal plains give way to hills, broken terrain	mountains with central plateau and Arctic slope	plateau in the N, Grand Canyon; desert in the SW	eastern delta and prairie, southern lowland forests, northwestern highlands
Capital:	Montgomery	Juneau	Phoenix	Little Rock

Economy

	Alabama	Alaska	Arizona	Arkansas
Industries:	pulp & paper, chemical, electronics, textiles	petroleum, tourism, fishing, mining, forestry, transportation, aerospace	manufacturing, construction, tourism, mining, agriculture, printing & publishing	manufacturing, agriculture, tourism, forestry
Manufactured Goods:	electronics, cast iron & plastic pipes, fabricated steel products, ships, paper products, poultry processing, furniture, tires	fish products, lumber & pulp, furs	electronics, metals, aircraft and missiles, clothing	food products, chemicals, lumber, paper, plastics, furniture, auto and airplane parts, clothing, machinery, steel
Farm Products:	cattle, hogs, chickens; cotton, peanuts, sweet potatoes, potatoes, other vegetables	cattle, hogs; greenhouse products, barley, oats, hay, potatoes, lettuce, aquaculture	cattle, sheep, hogs; cotton, lettuce, cauliflower, broccoli, sorghum, barley, corn, wheat, citrus fruits	cattle, hogs, chickens; rice, soybeans, cotton, tomatoes, grapes, apples, vegetables, peaches, wheat
Employment:	23.9% service; 23.1% trade; 18.7% manufacturing; 18.6% government	26.6% government; 25.7% service; 20.4% trade; 4.6% manufacturing	32.0% service; 23.4% trade; 16.0% government; 9.5% manufacturing	31.7% manufacturing; 23.9% service; 22.9% trade; 16.6% government

Fun Facts

	Alabama	Alaska	Arizona	Arkansas
State Date:	December 14, 1819	January 3, 1959	February 14, 1912	June 15, 1836
Motto:	We dare defend our rights.	North to the future	God enriches.	The people rule.
Flower:	Camellia	Forget-Me-Not	Blossom of the Saguaro Cactus	Apple Blossom
Bird:	Yellowhammer	Willow Ptarmigan	Paloverde	Mockingbird
Tree:	Southern Longleaf Pine	Sitka Spruce	Cactus Wren	Pine
Song:	Alabama	Alaska's Flag	Arizona	Arkansas
Nickname(s):	Heart of Dixieland, Camellia State	The Last Frontier (unofficial)	Grand Canyon State	The Natural State, The Razorback State
Web Site:	alaweb.asc.edu	state.ak.us	state.az.us	state.ar.us

California Colorado Connecticut Delaware

People (2000)

California	Colorado	Connecticut	Delaware
Population: 33,871,648	**Population:** 4,301,261	**Population:** 3,405,565	**Population:** 783,600
Population Density: 217.2 people per square mile	**Population Density:** 41.5 people per square mile	**Population Density:** 702.9 people per square mile	**Population Density:** 401.1 people per square mile
Racial Distribution: 59.5% white; 6.7% black; 1.0% Native American; 11.2% Asian/Pacific Islander; 32.4% Hispanic	**Racial Distribution:** 82.8% white; 3.8% black; 1.0% Native American; 2.3% Asian/Pacific Islander; 17.1% Hispanic	**Racial Distribution:** 81.6% white; 9.1% black; 0.3% Native American; 2.5% Asian/Pacific Islander; 9.4% Hispanic	**Racial Distribution:** 74.6% white; 19.2% black; 0.3% Native American; 2.1% Asian/Pacific Islander; 4.8% Hispanic

Geography

California	Colorado	Connecticut	Delaware
Total Area: 163,696 square miles	**Total Area:** 104,094 square miles	**Total Area:** 5,543 square miles	**Total Area:** 2,489 square miles
Climate: moderate temperatures and rainfall along the coast; extremes in the interior	**Climate:** low humidity; abundant sunshine; wide daily/seasonal temperature ranges; alpine conditions	**Climate:** moderate; winters slightly below freezing; warm, humid summers	**Climate:** moderate
Topography: mountainous coastline, central valley, mountains to E and N, desert basins in southern interior	**Topography:** high plains, hilly/mountainous central plateau; western mountains, wide valleys, deep canyons	**Topography:** western uplands; narrow central lowland; hilly eastern upland drained by rivers	**Topography:** Piedmont plateau sloping to near sea-level plain
Capital: Sacramento	**Capital:** Denver	**Capital:** Hartford	**Capital:** Dover

Economy

California	Colorado	Connecticut	Delaware
Industries: agriculture, tourism, electronics, telecommunications, entertainment	**Industries:** construction, government, tourism, agriculture, aerospace, electronics	**Industries:** manufacturing, trade, government, finance	**Industries:** chemical, agriculture, finance, fishing, tourism, auto assembly, food processing, transportation
Manufactured Goods: electronic equipment, computers	**Manufactured Goods:** computers, aerospace products	**Manufactured Goods:** aircraft engines and parts, submarines, helicopters, computers, electronic equipment, medical instruments, pharmaceuticals/drugs	**Manufactured Goods:** nylon, clothing, luggage, autos, processed meats and vegetables, train/aircraft equipment
Farm Products: cattle, sheep, hogs, chickens; grapes, cotton, flowers, oranges, rice, nursery products, hay, tomatoes, lettuce, strawberries, almonds, asparagus; milk and cream	**Farm Products:** cattle, sheep, hogs, chickens; corn, wheat, hay, sugar beets, barley, potatoes, apples, peaches, pears, dry beans, sorghum, onions, oats, sunflowers, vegetables	**Farm Products:** cattle, hogs, chickens; nursery plants, vegetables, tobacco, apples	**Farm Products:** cattle, hogs, chickens; soybeans, potatoes, vegetables, barley, wheat, corn, sorghum
Employment: 31.4% service; 22.7% trade; 16.3% government; 13.4% manufacturing	**Employment:** 30.6% service; 23.7% trade; 15.5% government; 9.2% manufacturing	**Employment:** 31.7% service; 21.5% trade; 15.6% manufacturing; 14.5% government	**Employment:** 28.4% service; 21.9% trade; 13.8% manufacturing; 13.8% government

Fun Facts

California	Colorado	Connecticut	Delaware
State Date: September 9, 1850	**State Date:** August 1, 1876	**State Date:** January 9, 1788	**State Date:** December 7, 1787
Motto: Eureka (I have found it.)	**Motto:** Nothing without Providence	**Motto:** He who transplanted still sustains.	**Motto:** Liberty and independence
Flower: Golden Poppy	**Flower:** Rocky Mountain Columbine	**Flower:** Mountain Laurel	**Flower:** Peach Blossom
Bird: California Valley Quail	**Bird:** Lark Bunting	**Bird:** American Robin	**Bird:** Blue Hen Chicken
Tree: California Redwood	**Tree:** Colorado Blue Spruce	**Tree:** White Oak	**Tree:** American Holly
Song: I Love You, California	**Song:** Where the Columbines Grow	**Song:** Yankee Doodle	**Song:** Our Delaware
Nickname: Golden State	**Nickname:** Centennial State	**Nicknames:** Constitution State, Nutmeg State	**Nicknames:** First State, Diamond State
Web Site: state.ca.us	**Web Site:** state.co.us	**Web Site:** state.ct.us	**Web Site:** state.de.us

| Florida | Georgia | Hawaii | Idaho |

People (2000)

Population: 15,982.378
Population Density:
296.4 people per square mile
Racial Distribution:
78.0% white; 14.6% black;
0.3% Native American;
1.8% Asian/Pacific Islander;
16.8% Hispanic

Population: 8,168,453
Population Density:
141.4 people per square mile
Racial Distribution:
65.1% white; 28.7% black;
0.3% Native American;
2.2% Asian/Pacific Islander;
5.3% Hispanic

Population: 1,211,537
Population Density:
188.6 people per square mile
Racial Distribution:
24.3% white; 1.8% black;
0.3% Native American;
51.0% Asian/Pacific Islander;
7.2% Hispanic

Population: 1,293,953
Population Density:
15.6 people per square mile
Racial Distribution:
91.0% white; 0.4% black;
1.4% Native American;
1.0% Asian/Pacific Islander;
7.9% Hispanic

Geography

Total Area: 65,755 square
miles
Climate: subtropical N,
tropical S
Topography: flat or rolling
land
Capital: Tallahassee

Total Area: 59,425 square
miles
Climate: tropical in summer;
cold in winter
Topography: mountains;
central piedmont to fall line
of rivers; coastal plain
Capital: Atlanta

Total Area: 10,931 square
miles
Climate: subtropical with
wide variations in rainfall
Topography: islands that are
tops of partially submerged
volcanic mountains; two
active volcanoes
Capital: Honolulu

Total Area: 83,570 square
miles
Climate: moderate with west-
erly winds; drier, colder in SE
Topography: plains in the S;
central region of mountains,
canyons, gorges
Capital: Boise

Economy

Industries: tourism, agriculture, manufacturing, con-
struction, services, printing
and publishing
Manufactured Goods: electronic equipment, transportation equipment, chemicals,
industrial machinery
Farm Products: cattle, hogs,
chickens; citrus fruits, vegetables, melons, potatoes,
sugarcane, strawberries
Employment: 37.6% service;
24.5% trade; 14.2% government; 6.8% manufacturing

Industries: services,
manufacturing, trade
Manufactured Goods:
textiles, processed food,
pulp and paper products
Farm Products: cattle, hogs,
chickens; peanuts, cotton,
corn, tobacco, hay, soybeans
Employment: 27.5% service;
25.2% trade; 15.3% government; 15.1% manufacturing

Industries: tourism, agriculture, printing and publishing
Manufactured Goods:
processed sugar, canned
pineapple, clothing
Farm Products: cattle, hogs,
chickens; sugar, pineapples,
macadamia nuts, tropical
fruits, coffee, vegetables,
flowers
Employment: 32.5% service;
24.8% trade; 21.2% government; 3.1% manufacturing

Industries: manufacturing,
agriculture, tourism, lumber,
mining, electronics
Manufactured Goods: computers, lumber/wood prod-
ucts, chemicals, metals
Farm Products: cattle, sheep,
hogs, chickens; potatoes,
peas, dry beans, sugar beets,
alfalfa seed, wheat, hops,
barley, plums, mint, onions,
corn, cherries, apples, hay
Employment: 25.4% service;
24.8% trade; 19.5% government; 13.8% manufacturing

Fun Facts

State Date: March 3, 1845
Motto: In God we trust
Flower: Orange Blossom
Bird: Mockingbird
Tree: Sabal Palmetto Palm
Song: Old Folks at Home
Nickname: Sunshine State
Web Site: state.fl.us

State Date: January 2, 1788
Motto: Wisdom, justice, and
moderation
Flower: Cherokee Rose
Bird: Brown Thrasher
Tree: Live Oak
Song: Georgia on My Mind
Nicknames: Empire State of
the South, Peach State
Web Site: state.ga.us

State Date: August 21, 1959
Motto: The life of the land is
perpetuated in righteousness.
Flower: Yellow Hibiscus
Bird: Hawaiian Goose (Nene)
Tree: Kukui (Candlenut)
Song: Hawaii Ponoi
Nickname: Aloha State
Web Site: hawaii.gov

State Date: July 3, 1890
Motto: It is perpetual.
Flower: Syringa
Bird: Mountain Bluebird
Tree: White Pine
Song: Here We Have Idaho
Nickname: Gem State
Web Site: state.id.us

Illinois	Indiana	Iowa	Kansas

People (2000)

Illinois	Indiana	Iowa	Kansas
Population: 12,419,293	**Population:** 6,080,485	**Population:** 2,926,324	**Population:** 2,668,418
Population Density: 223.4 people per square mile	**Population Density:** 169.5 people per square mile	**Population Density:** 52.4 people per square mile	**Population Density:** 32.9 people per square mile
Racial Distribution: 73.5% white; 15.1% black; 0.2% Native American; 3.4% Asian/Pacific Islander; 12.3% Hispanic	**Racial Distribution:** 87.5% white; 8.4% black; 0.3% Native American; 1.0% Asian/Pacific Islander; 3.5% Hispanic	**Racial Distribution:** 93.9% white; 2.1% black; 0.3% Native American; 1.3% Asian/Pacific Islander; 2.8% Hispanic	**Racial Distribution:** 86.1% white; 5.7% black; 0.9% Native American; 1.8% Asian/Pacific Islander; 7.0% Hispanic

Geography

Illinois	Indiana	Iowa	Kansas
Total Area: 57,914 square miles	**Total Area:** 36,418 square miles	**Total Area:** 56,272 square miles	**Total Area:** 82,277 square miles
Climate: cold, snowy winters and hot summers	**Climate:** four distinct seasons	**Climate:** humid summers	**Climate:** great extremes between summer and winter
Topography: prairie and fertile plains throughout; open hills in the southern region	**Topography:** hilly southern region; fertile rolling plains in central region; dunes along Lake Michigan shore	**Topography:** watershed from NW to SE; flat land in north-central area	**Topography:** hilly plains in the E; level prairie and hills in central area; high plains in the W
Capital: Springfield	**Capital:** Indianapolis	**Capital :** Des Moines	**Capital:** Topeka

Economy

Illinois	Indiana	Iowa	Kansas
Industries: services, manufacturing, travel, trade, finance, construction, health care, agriculture, printing and publishing	**Industries:** manufacturing, services, agriculture, government, trade, transportation	**Industries:** agriculture, communications, construction, finance, trade, manufacturing	**Industries:** manufacturing, finance, services, printing and publishing
Manufactured Goods: machinery, electronic equipment, metals, chemicals	**Manufactured Goods:** metals, automobiles, industrial machinery, electronics	**Manufactured Goods:** processed foods, tires, farm machinery, electronic products, appliances, furniture, chemicals, fertilizers, auto accessories	**Manufactured Goods:** transportation equipment, machinery, computer equipment, processed foods
Farm Products: cattle, sheep, hogs, chickens; corn, soybeans, wheat, sorghum, hay	**Farm Products:** cattle, sheep, hogs, chickens; corn, soybeans, wheat, nursery and greenhouse products, vegetables, fruit, hay, tobacco, mint	**Farm Products:** cattle, sheep, hogs, chickens; corn, soybeans, oats, hay	**Farm Products:** cattle, sheep, hogs, chickens; wheat, sorghum, corn, hay, soybeans, sunflowers
Employment: 30.7% service; 22.4% trade; 15.8% manufacturing; 14.1% government	**Employment:** 24.9% service; 23.4% trade; 23.0% manufacturing; 13.8% government	**Employment:** 26.4% service; 24.1% trade; 17.6% manufacturing; 16.4% government	**Employment:** 26.0% service; 24.0% trade; 18.1% government; 15.7% manufacturing

Fun Facts

Illinois	Indiana	Iowa	Kansas
State Date: December 3, 1818	**State Date:** December 11, 1816	**State Date:** December 28, 1846	**State Date:** January 29, 1861
Motto: State sovereignty, national union	**Motto:** Crossroads of America	**Motto:** Our liberties we prize, and our rights we will maintain.	**Motto:** To the stars through difficulties
Flower: Native Violet	**Flower:** Peony	**Flower:** Wild Rose	**Flower:** Native Sunflower
Bird: Cardinal	**Bird:** Cardinal	**Bird:** Eastern Goldfinch	**Bird:** Western Meadowlark
Tree: White Oak	**Tree:** Tulip Poplar	**Tree:** Oak	**Tree:** Cottonwood
Song: Illinois	**Song:** On the Banks of the Wabash	**Song:** The Song of Iowa	**Song:** Home on the Range
Nickname: Prairie State	**Nickname:** Hoosier State	**Nickname:** Hawkeye State	**Nickname:** Sunflower State
Web Site: state.il.us	**Web Site:** ai.org	**Web Site:** state.ia.us	**Web Site:** ink.org

Kentucky   Louisiana   Maine   Maryland

People (2000)

Population: 4,041,769
Population Density:
101.7 people per square mile
Racial Distribution:
90.1% white; 7.3% black;
0.2% Native American;
0.7% Asian/Pacific Islander;
1.5% Hispanic

Population: 4,468,976
Population Density:
102.6 people per square mile
Racial Distribution:
63.9% white; 32.5% black;
0.6% Native American;
1.2% Asian/Pacific Islander;
2.4% Hispanic

Population: 1,274,923
Population Density:
41.3 people per square mile
Racial Distribution:
96.9% white; 0.5% black;
0.6% Native American;
0.7% Asian/Pacific Islander;
0.7% Hispanic

Population: 5,296,486
Population Density:
541.9 people per square mile
Racial Distribution:
64.0% white; 27.9% black;
0.3% Native American;
4.0% Asian/Pacific Islander;
4.3% Hispanic

Geography

Total Area: 40,409 square miles
Climate: moderate, with plentiful rainfall
Topography: mountainous in the E; rounded hills in the N; bluegrass plains; wooded rocky hillsides
Capital: Frankfort

Total Area: 49,651 square miles
Climate: subtropical
Topography: mashes and river flood plain; valley lowlands; upland hills
Capital: Baton Rouge

Total Area: 35,385 square miles
Climate: mild summers; cold, harsh winters averaging over 100" of snow
Topography: mountains and rugged terrain in the W; sandy/rocky coast with peninsulas and fjords
Capital: Augusta

Total Area: 12,407 square miles
Climate: moderate in the W; humid subtropical in the E
Topography: coastal plain and piedmont plateau
Capital: Annapolis

Economy

Industries: manufacturing, services, finance, trade, printing and publishing
Manufactured Goods: transportation and industrial machinery, clothing, electronic equipment
Farm Products: cattle, hogs, chickens; tobacco, corn, soybeans
Employment: 26.0% service; 23.7% trade; 17.5% manufacturing; 17% government

Industries: trade, tourism, manufacturing, construction, transportation, communication, finance, mining
Manufactured Goods: chemicals, transportation equipment, electronics, petroleum products, lumber, paper
Farm Products: cattle, hogs, chickens; soybeans, sugarcane, rice, corn, cotton, sweet potatoes, pecans
Employment: 27.8% service; 23% trade; 19.8% government; 9.7% manufacturing

Industries: manufacturing, agriculture, fishing, services, trade, government, finance, construction
Manufactured Goods: paper and wood products, transportation equipment
Farm Products: cattle, hogs, chickens; potatoes, fish and shellfish
Employment: 30.0% service; 24.9% trade; 16.8% government; 14.2% manufacturing

Industries: manufacturing, biotechnology and information technology, services, tourism
Manufactured Goods: electronic equipment, processed foods, chemicals, printed materials
Farm Products: cattle, hogs, chickens; greenhouse and nursery products, soybeans, corn
Employment: 34.1% service; 22.9% trade; 18.7% government; 7.3% manufacturing

Fun Facts

State Date: June 1, 1792
Motto: United we stand, divided we fall.
Flower: Goldenrod
Bird: Cardinal
Tree: Tulip Poplar
Song: My Old Kentucky Home
Nickname: Bluegrass State
Web Site: state.ky.us

State Date: April 30, 1812
Motto: Union, justice, and confidence
Flower: Magnolia
Bird: Eastern Brown Pelican
Tree: Cypress
Song: Give Me Louisiana
Nickname: Pelican State
Web Site: state.la.us

State Date: March 15, 1820
Motto: I direct.
Flower: White Pine Cone and Tassel
Bird: Chickadee
Tree: Eastern White Pine
Song: State of Maine Song
Nickname: Pine Tree State
Web Site: state.me.us

State Date: April 28, 1788
Motto: Manly deeds, womanly words
Flower: Black-eyed Susan
Bird: Baltimore Oriole
Tree: White Oak
Song: Maryland, My Maryland
Nickname: Old Line State
Web Site: state.md.us

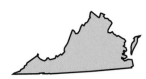

Massachusetts   Michigan   Minnesota   Mississippi

People (2000)

Population: 6,349,097	**Population:** 9,938,444	**Population:** 4,919,479	**Population:** 2,844.658
Population Density: 809.8 people per square mile	**Population Density:** 175.0 people per square mile	**Population Density:** 61.8 people per square mile	**Population Density:** 60.6 people per square mile
Racial Distribution: 84.5% white; 5.4% black; 0.2% Native American; 3.8% Asian/Pacific Islander; 6.8% Hispanic	**Racial Distribution:** 80.2% white; 14.2% black; 0.6% Native American; 1.8% Asian/Pacific Islander; 3.3% Hispanic	**Racial Distribution:** 89.4% white; 3.5% black; 1.1% Native American; 2.9% Asian/Pacific Islander; 2.9% Hispanic	**Racial Distribution:** 61.4% white; 36.3% black; 0.4% Native American; 0.7% Asian/Pacific Islander; 1.4% Hispanic

Geography

Total Area: 10,555 square miles	**Total Area:** 96,716 square miles	**Total Area:** 86,943 square miles	**Total Area:** 48,430 square miles
Climate: moderate; warm, humid summers and cold winters	**Climate:** four seasons	**Climate:** moist Great Lakes storm belt; semiarid plains to the W	**Climate:** semitropical, with abundant rainfall
Topography: jagged, indented coast; flat land yields to stony upland pastures near central region and gentle hills in W	**Topography:** low rolling hills in S to northern tableland of hills; level in NE with swampy areas; higher, rugged terrain in W	**Topography:** lakes covering about half the state; rocky ridges in NE; flat plain in NW; rolling plains and deep river valleys in S	**Topography:** low, fertile delta; sandy gulf coastal terraces followed by piney woods and prairie
Capital: Boston	**Capital:** Lansing	**Capital:** St. Paul	**Capital:** Jackson

Economy

Industries: services, trade, manufacturing, printing and publishing	**Industries:** manufacturing, services, tourism, agriculture, forestry/lumber	**Industries:** forestry, mining, manufacturing, tourism, printing and publishing	**Industries:** warehousing and distribution, services, manufacturing, government, trade
Manufactured Goods: electronic equipment, industrial machinery, fabricated metal products	**Manufactured Goods:** automobiles, machinery, metals, plastics, office furniture	**Manufactured Goods:** chemicals, paper, machinery, electronic equipment, computers, medical instruments, metals	**Manufactured Goods:** chemicals, plastics, processed foods, furniture, lumber and wood products, electrical machinery, transportation equipment
Farm Products: cattle, hogs, chickens; cranberries, vegetables	**Farm Products:** cattle, sheep, hogs, chickens; corn, wheat, soybeans, dry beans, hay, potatoes, sweet corn, apples, cherries, sugar beets, blueberries, cucumbers, grapes	**Farm Products:** cattle, sheep, hogs, chickens; corn, soybeans, wheat, sugar beets, hay, barley, potatoes, sunflowers	**Farm Products:** cattle, sheep, hogs, chickens; cotton, rice, soybeans
Employment: 36.0% service; 22.5% trade; 13.2% government; 13.1% manufacturing	**Employment:** 27.6% service; 23.4% trade; 21.2% manufacturing; 15.0% government	**Employment:** 29.2% service; 23.7% trade; 16.6% manufacturing; 14.9% government	**Employment:** 23.6% service; 21.3% trade; 20.9% manufacturing; 20.4% government

Fun Facts

State Date: February 6, 1788	**State Date:** January 26, 1837	**State Date:** May 11, 1858	**State Date:** December 10, 1817
Motto: By the sword we seek peace, but peace only under liberty.	**Motto:** If you seek a pleasant peninsula, look about you.	**Motto:** The star of the north	**Motto:** By valor and arms
Flower: Mayflower	**Flower:** Apple Blossom	**Flower:** Pink and White Lady's-Slipper	**Flower:** Magnolia
Bird: Chickadee	**Bird:** Robin	**Bird:** Common Loon	**Bird:** Mockingbird
Tree: American Elm	**Tree:** White Pine	**Tree:** Red Pine	**Tree:** Magnolia
Song: All Hail to Massachusetts	**Song:** Michigan, My Michigan	**Song:** Hail! Minnesota	**Song:** Go, Mississippi
Nickname: Bay State	**Nicknames:** Great Lakes State, Wolverine State	**Nicknames:** North Star State, Gopher State	**Nickname:** Magnolia State
Web Site: state.ma.us	**Web Site:** state.mi.us	**Web Site:** state.mn.us	**Web Site:** state.ms.us

Missouri   Montana   Nebraska   Nevada

People (2000)

Missouri	**Montana**	**Nebraska**	**Nevada**
Population: 5,595,211	**Population:** 902,195	**Population:** 1,711,263	**Population:** 1,998,257
Population Density: 81.2 people per square mile	**Population Density:** 6.2 people per square mile	**Population Density:** 22.3 people per square mile	**Population Density:** 18.2 people per square mile
Racial Distribution: 84.9% white; 11.2% black; 0.4% Native American; 1.2% Asian/Pacific Islander; 2.1% Hispanic	**Racial Distribution:** 90.6% white; 0.3% black; 6.2% Native American; 0.6% Asian/Pacific Islander; 2.0% Hispanic	**Racial Distribution:** 89.6% white; 4.0% black; 0.9% Native American; 1.4% Asian/Pacific Islander; 5.5% Hispanic	**Racial Distribution:** 75.2% white; 6.8% black; 1.3% Native American; 4.9% Asian/Pacific Islander; 19.7% Hispanic

Geography

Total Area: 69,704 square miles	**Total Area:** 147,042 square miles	**Total Area:** 77,354 square miles	**Total Area:** 110,561 square miles
Climate: periods of cold air, moist and warm air, and drier air	**Climate:** cold with low humidity	**Climate:** semi-arid	**Climate:** semiarid and arid
Topography: rolling hills; open, fertile plains; prairies	**Topography:** mountains in western third of the state; gently rolling plains in rest of state	**Topography:** plains and hills	**Topography:** rugged mountain ranges; desert
Capital: Jefferson City	**Capital:** Helena	**Capital:** Lincoln	**Capital:** Carson City

Economy

Industries: agriculture, manufacturing, aerospace, tourism	**Industries:** agriculture, timber, mining, tourism, oil and gas, printing and publishing	**Industries:** agriculture, manufacturing	**Industries:** tourism, mining, manufacturing, government, retailing, warehousing, trucking
Manufactured Goods: transportation equipment, processed foods, electronic equipment, chemicals	**Manufactured Goods:** wood and paper products, metals, petroleum and coal products	**Manufactured Goods:** processed foods, industrial machinery, printed materials, electronic equipment, metal products	**Manufactured Goods:** food products, plastics, chemicals, aerospace products, irrigation equipment
Farm Products: cattle, sheep, hogs, chickens; soybeans, corn, wheat, hay	**Farm Products:** cattle, sheep, hogs, chickens; wheat, barley, sugar beets, hay, oats	**Farm Products:** cattle, sheep, hogs, chickens; corn, sorghum, soybeans, hay, wheat, dry beans, oats, potatoes, sugar beets	**Farm Products:** cattle, sheep, hogs; hay, alfalfa seed, potatoes, onions, garlic, barley, wheat
Employment: 28.4% service; 23.7% trade; 15.6% government; 14.7% manufacturing	**Employment:** 29.7% service; 26.3% trade; 21.0% government; 6.3% manufacturing	**Employment:** 27.0% service; 24.0% trade; 17.6% government; 13.1% manufacturing	**Employment:** 43.3% service; 20.5% trade; 12.2% government; 4.2% manufacturing

Fun Facts

State Date: August 10, 1821	**State Date:** November 8, 1889	**State Date:** March 1, 1867	**State Date:** October 31, 1864
Motto: The welfare of the people shall be the supreme law.	**Motto:** Gold and silver	**Motto:** Equality before the law	**Motto:** All for our country
Flower: Hawthorn	**Flower:** Bitterroot	**Flower:** Goldenrod	**Flower:** Sagebrush
Bird: Bluebird	**Bird:** Western Meadowlark	**Bird:** Western Meadowlark	**Bird:** Mountain Bluebird
Tree: Dogwood	**Tree:** Ponderosa Pine	**Tree:** Cottonwood	**Trees:** Single-Leaf Piñon, Bristle-Cone Pine
Song: Missouri Waltz	**Song:** Montana	**Song:** Beautiful Nebraska	**Song:** Home Means Nevada
Nickname: Show Me State	**Nickname:** Treasure State	**Nickname:** Cornhusker State	**Nicknames:** Sagebrush State, Battle Born State, Silver State
Web Site: state.mo.us	**Web Site:** mt.gov	**Web Site:** state.ne.us	**Web Site:** state.nv.us

New Hampshire New Jersey New Mexico New York

People (2000)

New Hampshire	New Jersey	New Mexico	New York
Population: 1,235,786	**Population:** 8,414,350	**Population:** 1,819,046	**Population:** 18,976,457
Population Density: 137.8 people per square mile	**Population Density:** 1,134.5 people per square mile	**Population Density:** 15.0 people per square mile	**Population Density:** 401.9 people per square mile
Racial Distribution: 96.0% white; 0.7% black; 0.2% Native American; 1.3% Asian/Pacific Islander; 1.7% Hispanic	**Racial Distribution:** 72.6% white; 13.6% black; 0.2% Native American; 5.7% Asian/Pacific Islander; 13.3% Hispanic	**Racial Distribution:** 66.8% white; 1.9% black; 9.5% Native American; 1.2% Asian/Pacific Islander; 42.1% Hispanic	**Racial Distribution:** 67.9% white; 15.9% black; 0.4% Native American; 5.6% Asian/Pacific Islander; 15.1% Hispanic

Geography

New Hampshire	New Jersey	New Mexico	New York
Total Area: 9,350 square miles	**Total Area:** 8,721 square miles	**Total Area:** 121,589 square miles	**Total Area:** 54,556 square miles
Climate: highly varied, due to nearby high mountains and ocean	**Climate:** moderate, with marked difference between NW and SE	**Climate:** dry, with temperatures rising/falling 5 degrees for every 1,000 feet of elevation	**Climate:** variable due to nearby ocean
Topography: low, rolling coast followed by hills and mountains rising out of a central plateau	**Topography:** mountain peaks and valleys; flat-topped NE-SW mountain ranges; low plains broken by high ridges; coastal plain	**Topography:** plains, mountains, high plateau	**Topography:** highest and most rugged mountains in the NE region; lowland river basin, coastal plain
Capital: Concord	**Capital:** Trenton	**Capital:** Santa Fe	**Capital:** Albany

Economy

New Hampshire	New Jersey	New Mexico	New York
Industries: tourism, manufacturing, agriculture, trade, mining	**Industries:** pharmaceuticals, telecommunications, biotechnology, printing and publishing	**Industries:** government, services, trade	**Industries:** manufacturing, finance, publishing, tourism, transportation
Manufactured Goods: machinery, electronic products, plastics, fabricated metal products	**Manufactured Goods:** chemicals, electronic equipment, processed food	**Manufactured Goods:** processed food, machinery, clothing, lumber, printing, electronics, semiconductors	**Manufactured Goods:** books, magazines, clothing, sporting goods, electronic equipment, auto and aircraft parts
Farm Products: cattle, hogs, chickens; dairy products, nursery and greenhouse products, hay, vegetables, fruit, maple syrup/sugar products	**Farm Products:** cattle, hogs, chickens; nursery and greenhouse products, tomatoes, blueberries, peaches, peppers, cranberries, soybeans	**Farm Products:** cattle, sheep, hogs; hay, onions, chilis, greenhouse and nursery products, pecans, cotton	**Farm Products:** cattle, sheep, hogs, chickens; fruits, onions, potatoes, vegetables, corn, hay, wheat, oats, maple syrup, wine; milk, cheese
Employment: 29.4% service; 26.3% trade; 17.2% manufacturing; 13.8% government	**Employment:** 32.7% service; 23.5% trade; 14.9% government; 11.8% manufacturing	**Employment:** 29.0% service; 24.9% government; 23.3% trade; 5.7% manufacturing	**Employment:** 35.0% service; 20.2% trade; 17.2% government; 10.2% manufacturing

Fun Facts

New Hampshire	New Jersey	New Mexico	New York
State Date: June 21, 1788	**State Date:** December 18, 1787	**State Date:** January 2, 1912	**State Date:** July 26, 1788
Motto: Live free or die.	**Motto:** Liberty and prosperity	**Motto:** It grows as it goes.	**Motto:** Ever upward
Flower: Purple Lilac	**Flower:** Purple Violet	**Flower:** Yucca	**Flower:** Rose
Bird: Purple Finch	**Bird:** Eastern Goldfinch	**Bird:** Roadrunner	**Bird:** Bluebird
Tree: White Birch	**Tree:** Red Oak	**Tree:** Piñon	**Tree:** Sugar Maple
Song: Old New Hampshire	**Song:** I'm from New Jersey	**Song:** O, Fair New Mexico	**Song:** I Love New York
Nickname: Granite State	**Nickname:** Garden State	**Nickname:** Land of Enchantment	**Nickname:** Empire State
Web Site: state.nh.us	**Web Site:** state.nj.us	**Web Site:** state.nm.us	**Web Site:** empire.state.ny.us

People (2000)

Population: 8,049,313	**Population:** 642,200	**Population:** 11,353,140	**Population:** 3,450,654
Population Density: 165.2 people per square mile	**Population Density:** 9.3 people per square mile	**Population Density:** 277.3 people per square mile	**Population Density:** 50.3 people per square mile
Racial Distribution: 72.1% white; 21.6% black; 1.2% Native American; 1.5% Asian/Pacific Islander; 4.7% Hispanic	**Racial Distribution:** 92.4% white; 0.6% black; 4.9% Native American; 0.6% Asian/Pacific Islander; 1.2% Hispanic	**Racial Distribution:** 85.0% white; 11.5% black; 0.2% Native American; 1.2% Asian/Pacific Islander; 1.9% Hispanic	**Racial Distribution:** 76.2% white; 7.8% black; 7.6% Native American; 1.4% Asian/Pacific Islander; 5.2% Hispanic

Geography

Total Area: 53,819 square miles	**Total Area:** 70,700 square miles	**Total Area:** 44,825 square miles	**Total Area:** 69,898 square miles
Climate: subtropical in SE; moderate in mountainous area	**Climate:** wide range of temperature and moderate rainfall	**Climate:** variable; much precipitation	**Climate:** humid eastern and dry western zones
Topography: coastal plain and tidewater; piedmont plateau; gentle to rugged hills; mountains	**Topography:** prairie and plains	**Topography:** rolling plains	**Topography:** high plains in the W; hills and small mountains in the E; river basin and plains
Capital: Raleigh	**Capital:** Bismarck	**Capital:** Columbus	**Capital:** Oklahoma City

Economy

Industries: manufacturing, agriculture, tourism	**Industries:** agriculture, mining, tourism, manufacturing, telecommunications	**Industries:** manufacturing, trade, services	**Industries:** manufacturing, mineral and energy exploration, agriculture, services
Manufactured Goods: processed foods, textiles, industrial machinery, electronic equipment, furniture, tobacco products	**Manufactured Goods:** farm equipment, processed foods, fabricated metals, electronics	**Manufactured Goods:** transportation equipment, machinery, metal products	**Manufactured Goods:** nonelectrical machinery, transportation equipment, processed foods, metal products
Farm Products: cattle, hogs, chickens; tobacco, cotton, soybeans, corn, wheat, peanuts, sweet potatoes	**Farm Products:** cattle, sheep, hogs; wheat, durum, barley, flaxseed, oats, potatoes, dry beans, honey, soybeans, sugar beets, sunflowers, hay	**Farm Products:** cattle, sheep, hogs, chickens; corn, hay, wheat, oats, soybeans	**Farm Products:** cattle, sheep, hogs, chickens; wheat, cotton, hay, peanuts, sorghum, soybeans, corn, pecans
Employment: 26.1% service; 22.4% trade; 20.0% manufacturing; 16.1% government	**Employment:** 28.4% service; 25.0% trade; 22.4% government; 7.5% manufacturing	**Employment:** 28.0% service; 24.0% trade; 19.3% manufacturing; 14.3% government	**Employment:** 28.7% service; 22.9% trade; 19.6% government; 12.4% manufacturing

Fun Facts

State Date: November 21, 1789	**State Date:** November 2, 1889	**State Date:** March 1, 1803	**State Date:** November 16, 1907
Motto: To be rather than to seem	**Motto:** Liberty and union, now and forever, one and inseparable	**Motto:** With God, all things are possible.	**Motto:** Labor conquers all things.
Flower: Dogwood	**Flower:** Wild Prairie Rose	**Flower:** Scarlet Carnation	**Flower:** Mistletoe
Bird: Cardinal	**Bird:** Western Meadowlark	**Bird:** Cardinal	**Bird:** Scissor-tailed Flycatcher
Tree: Pine	**Tree:** American Elm	**Tree:** Buckeye	**Tree:** Redbud
Song: The Old North State	**Song:** North Dakota Hymn	**Song:** Beautiful Ohio	**Song:** Oklahoma!
Nicknames: Tar Heel State, Old North State	**Nickname:** Peace Garden State	**Nickname:** Buckeye State	**Nickname:** Sooner State
Web Site: state.nc.us	**Web Site:** state.nd.us	**Web Site:** state.oh.us	**Web Site:** state.ok.us

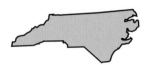

Oregon

Pennsylvania

Rhode Island

South Carolina

People (2000)

Population: 3,421,399
Population Density:
35.6 people per square mile
Racial Distribution:
86.6% white; 1.6% black;
1.3% Native American;
3.2% Asian/Pacific Islander;
8.0% Hispanic

Population: 12,281,054
Population Density:
274.0 people per square mile
Racial Distribution:
85.4% white; 10.0% black;
0.1% Native American;
1.8% Asian/Pacific Islander;
3.2% Hispanic

Population: 1,048,319
Population Density: 1,003.2
people per square mile
Racial Distribution:
85.0% white; 4.5% black;
0.5% Native American;
2.4% Asian/Pacific Islander;
8.7% Hispanic

Population: 4,021,012
Population Density:
133.2 people per square mile
Racial Distribution:
67.2% white; 29.5% black;
0.3% Native American;
0.9% Asian/Pacific Islander;
2.4% Hispanic

Geography

Total Area: 98,381 square miles
Climate: coastal mild and humid climate; dryness and extreme temperatures in central area
Topography: coastal range of rugged mountains; fertile river valley; volcanic peaks; plateau
Capital: Salem

Total Area: 46,055 square miles
Climate: wide range of seasonal temperatures
Topography: mountains with piedmont and coastal plain; rugged plateau falls to lowland in N
Capital: Harrisburg

Total Area: 1,545 square miles
Climate: variable
Topography: eastern lowlands; western uplands of flat and rolling hills
Capital: Providence

Total Area: 32,020 square miles
Climate: humid subtropical
Topography: mountains; piedmont and coastal plain
Capital: Columbia

Economy

Industries: manufacturing, services, trade, finance, government, construction
Manufactured Goods: electronics and semiconductors, lumber and wood products, metals, transportation equipment, processed foods, paper
Farm Products: cattle, sheep, hogs, chickens; hay, wheat, grass seed, potatoes, onions, pears, mint
Employment: 27.2% service; 24.6% trade; 16.8% government; 15.1% manufacturing

Industries: agribusiness, manufacturing, biotechnology, printing and publishing
Manufactured Goods: metal products, rubber and plastics, electronics, chemicals, lumber/wood products, stone/clay/glass products
Farm Products: cattle, sheep, hogs, chickens; corn, hay, mushrooms, apples, potatoes, wheat, oats
Employment: 32.2% service; 22.3% trade; 16.5% manufacturing; 13.2% government

Industries: services, manufacturing
Manufactured Goods: costume jewelry, toys, textiles, electronics
Farm Products: cattle, hogs, chickens; nursery products, turf and vegetable production
Employment: 34.5% service; 22.6% trade; 15.5% manufacturing; 13.8% government

Industries: tourism, agriculture, manufacturing
Manufactured Goods: textiles, chemicals, machinery and metal products
Farm Products: cattle, hogs, chickens; tobacco, cotton, soybeans, corn, wheat, peaches, tomatoes
Employment: 24.6% service; 24.0% trade; 18.2% manufacturing; 17.6% government

Fun Facts

State Date: February 14, 1859
Motto: She flies with her own wings.
Flower: Oregon Grape
Bird: Western Meadowlark
Tree: Douglas Fir
Song: Oregon, My Oregon
Nickname: Beaver State
Web Site: state.or.us

State Date: December 12, 1787
Motto: Virtue, liberty, and independence
Flower: Mountain Laurel
Bird: Ruffed Grouse
Tree: Hemlock
Song: Pennsylvania
Nickname: Keystone State
Web Site: state.pa.us

State Date: May 29, 1790
Motto: Hope
Flower: Violet
Bird: Rhode Island Red
Tree: Red Maple
Song: Rhode Island
Nicknames: Little Rhody, Ocean State
Web Site: state.ri.us

State Date: May 23, 1788
Motto: While I breathe, I hope.
Flower: Yellow Jessamine
Bird: Carolina Wren
Tree: Palmetto
Song: Carolina
Nickname: Palmetto State
Web Site: state.sc.us

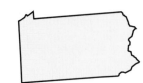

People (2000)

Population: 754,844	**Population:** 5,689,283	**Population:** 20,851,820	**Population:** 2,233,169
Population Density: 9.9 people per square mile	**Population Density:** 138.0 people per square mile	**Population Density:** 79.6 people per square mile	**Population Density:** 27.2 people per square mile
Racial Distribution: 88.7% white; 0.6% black; 8.3% Native American; 0.6% Asian/Pacific Islander; 1.4% Hispanic	**Racial Distribution:** 80.2% white; 16.4% black; 0.3% Native American; 1.0% Asian/Pacific Islander; 2.2% Hispanic	**Racial Distribution:** 71.0% white; 11.5% black; 0.6% Native American; 2.8% Asian/Pacific Islander; 32.0% Hispanic	**Racial Distribution:** 89.2% white; 0.8% black; 1.3% Native American; 2.4% Asian/Pacific Islander; 9.0% Hispanic

Geography

Total Area: 77,116 square miles	**Total Area:** 42,146 square miles	**Total Area:** 268,581 square miles	**Total Area:** 84,899 square miles
Climate: extremes of temperature, persistent winds, low precipitation and humidity	**Climate:** humid subtropical	**Climate:** extremely varied from dry to wet	**Climate:** arid; ranging from warm desert to alpine
Topography: prairie plains and rolling hills	**Topography:** mountains and valleys; plateaus; coastal plain with streams; a narrow strip of swamp and flood plain in the extreme W	**Topography:** coastal plain; inland plains broken by low mountains	**Topography:** brilliantly colored canyons; broad, flat, desert-like basin; mountains, valleys, and plateaus
Capital: Pierre	**Capital:** Nashville	**Capital:** Austin	**Capital:** Salt Lake City

Economy

Industries: agriculture, services, manufacturing	**Industries:** manufacturing, trade, services, tourism, finance, insurance, real estate, printing and publishing	**Industries:** manufacturing, trade, oil and gas, services	**Industries:** services, trade, manufacturing, government, transportation
Manufactured Goods: processed foods, machinery, electronic equipment	**Manufactured Goods:** chemicals, machinery, metal products, rubber/plastic products, paper products	**Manufactured Goods:** industrial machinery, electronic products, chemicals, clothing	**Manufactured Goods:** medical instruments, electronic components, processed foods, steel and copper
Farm Products: cattle, sheep, hogs, chickens; corn, soybeans, oats, wheat, sunflowers, sorghum	**Farm Products:** cattle, hogs, chickens; tobacco, cotton, soybeans, grain, corn	**Farm Products:** cattle, sheep, hogs, chickens; cotton, wheat, sorghum, vegetables, citrus and other fruits, greenhouse/nursery products, pecans, peanuts; milk, eggs	**Farm Products:** cattle, sheep, hogs, chickens; hay, corn, wheat, barley, apples, potatoes, cherries, onions, peaches, pears
Employment: 27.2% service; 24.1% trade; 19.5% government; 12.9% manufacturing	**Employment:** 27.0% service; 23.3% trade; 18.6% manufacturing; 15.0% government	**Employment:** 28.3% service; 23.8% trade; 17.2% government; 11.5% manufacturing	**Employment:** 28.2% service; 23.5% trade; 17.3% government; 12.5% manufacturing

Fun Facts

State Date: November 2, 1889	**State Date:** June 1, 1796	**State Date:** December 29, 1845	**State Date:** January 4, 1896
Motto: Under God, the people rule.	**Motto:** Agriculture and commerce	**Motto:** Friendship	**Motto:** Industry
Flower: Pasqueflower	**Flower:** Iris	**Flower:** Bluebonnet	**Flower:** Sego Lily
Bird: Chinese Ring-necked Pheasant	**Bird:** Mockingbird	**Bird:** Mockingbird	**Bird:** Seagull
Tree: Black Hills Spruce	**Tree:** Tulip Poplar	**Tree:** Pecan	**Tree:** Blue Spruce
Song: Hail, South Dakota	**Song:** Tennessee Waltz	**Song:** Texas, Our Texas	**Song:** Utah, We Love Thee
Nicknames: Coyote State, Mount Rushmore State	**Nickname:** Volunteer State	**Nickname:** Lone Star State	**Nickname:** Beehive State
Web Site: state.sd.us	**Web Site:** state.tn.us	**Web Site:** state.tx.us	**Web Site:** utah.com

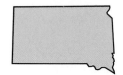
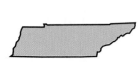

Vermont	Virginia	Washington	West Virginia

People (2000)

Vermont	Virginia	Washington	West Virginia
Population: 608,827	**Population:** 7,078,515	**Population:** 5,894,121	**Population:** 1,808,344
Population Density: 65.8 people per square mile	**Population Density:** 178.8 people per square mile	**Population Density:** 88.6 people per square mile	**Population Density:** 75.1 people per square mile
Racial Distribution: 96.8% white; 0.5% black; 0.4% Native American; 0.9% Asian/Pacific Islander; 0.9% Hispanic	**Racial Distribution:** 72.3% white; 19.6% black; 0.3% Native American; 3.8% Asian/Pacific Islander; 4.7% Hispanic	**Racial Distribution:** 81.8% white; 3.2% black; 1.6% Native American; 5.9% Asian/Pacific Islander; 7.5% Hispanic	**Racial Distribution:** 95.0% white; 3.2% black; 0.2% Native American; 0.5% Asian/Pacific Islander; 0.7% Hispanic

Geography

Vermont	Virginia	Washington	West Virginia
Total Area: 9,614 square miles	**Total Area:** 42,774 square miles	**Total Area:** 71,300 square miles	**Total Area:** 24,230 square miles
Climate: great temperature extremes; heavy snowfall in winter	**Climate:** mild	**Climate:** mild	**Climate:** humid except for coastal areas in the lower Panhandle area
Topography: mountainous	**Topography:** mountains and valleys; rolling piedmont plateau; tidewater, or coastal plain	**Topography:** mountains; open land along coast	**Topography:** ranging from hilly to mountainous
Capital: Montpelier	**Capital:** Richmond	**Capital:** Olympia	**Capital:** Charleston

Economy

Vermont	Virginia	Washington	West Virginia
Industries: manufacturing, tourism, agriculture, trade, finance, insurance, real estate, government	**Industries:** services, trade, government, manufacturing, tourism, agriculture	**Industries:** aerospace, biotechnology, international trade, forestry, tourism, agriculture, food processing	**Industries:** manufacturing, services, mining, tourism
Manufactured Goods: tools, furniture, books, computer components, specialty foods	**Manufactured Goods:** textiles, electrical equipment, industrial machinery, lumber and wood products, chemicals, rubber, plastics, furniture	**Manufactured Goods:** software, aircraft, pulp and paper, lumber and plywood, aluminum, processed fruits and vegetables, electronics	**Manufactured Goods:** machinery, plastic and hardwood products, metals, chemicals, automotive parts
Farm Products: cattle, hogs, chickens; dairy products, apples, maple syrup, greenhouse/nursery products, vegetables and small fruits	**Farm Products:** cattle, sheep, hogs, chickens; tobacco, grain, corn, soybeans, wheat, peanuts, cotton	**Farm Products:** cattle, sheep, hogs, chickens; apples, potatoes, hay	**Farm Products:** cattle, sheep, hogs, chickens; apples, peaches, hay, tobacco, corn, wheat, oats
Employment: 30.5% service; 22.9% trade; 16.6% government; 16.1% manufacturing	**Employment:** 32.2% service; 21.7% trade; 17.9% government; 11.4% manufacturing	**Employment:** 28.1% service; 24.1% trade; 18.1% government; 13.1% manufacturing	**Employment:** 29.8% service; 22.0% trade; 20.9% government; 10.9% manufacturing

Fun Facts

Vermont	Virginia	Washington	West Virginia
State Date: March 4, 1791	**State Date:** June 25, 1788	**State Date:** November 11, 1889	**State Date:** June 20, 1863
Motto: Freedom and unity	**Motto:** Thus always to tyrants	**Motto:** By and by	**Motto:** Mountaineers are always free.
Flower: Red Clover	**Flower:** Dogwood	**Flower:** Western Rhododendron	**Flower:** Big Rhododendron
Bird: Hermit Thrush	**Bird:** Cardinal	**Bird:** Willow Goldfinch	**Bird:** Cardinal
Tree: Sugar Maple	**Tree:** Dogwood	**Tree:** Western Hemlock	**Tree:** Sugar Maple
Song: These Green Mountains	**Song:** Carry Me Back to Old Virginia	**Song:** Washington, My Home	**Songs:** The West Virginia Hills; This Is My West Virginia; West Virginia, My Home
Nickname: Green Mountain State	**Nickname:** Old Dominion	**Nickname:** Evergreen State	**Nickname:** Mountain State
Web Site: state.vt.us	**Web Site:** state.va.us	**Web Site:** access.wa.gov	**Web Site:** state.wv.us

People (2000)

Population: 5,363,675	**Population:** 493,782
Population Density: 98.8 people per square mile	**Population Density:** 5.1 people per square mile
Racial Distribution: 88.9% white; 5.7% black; 0.9% Native American; 1.7% Asian/Pacific Islander; 3.6% Hispanic	**Racial Distribution:** 92.1% white; 0.8% black; 2.3% Native American; 0.7% Asian/Pacific Islander; 6.4% Hispanic

Geography

Total Area: 65,498 square miles	**Total Area:** 97,814 square miles
Climate: long, cold winters and short, warm summers	**Climate:** semi-desert conditions throughout; true desert in the Big Horn and Great Divide Basins
Topography: plains, limestone ridges, shallow lowlands	**Topography:** plains rising to foothills of Rocky Mountains
Capital: Madison	**Capital:** Cheyenne

Economy

Industries: manufacturing, trade, government, agriculture, tourism	**Industries:** mineral mining, tourism, agriculture
Manufactured Goods: motor vehicles, paper products, medical supplies, plastics	**Manufactured Goods:** refined petroleum, electronic devices, sporting goods, aircraft
Farm Products: cattle, sheep, hogs, chickens; corn, hay, soybeans, potatoes, cranberries, sweet corn, peas, oats, snap beans; milk, butter, cheese	**Farm Products:** cattle, sheep, hogs, chickens; wheat, beans, barley, oats, sugar beets, hay
Employment: 26.5% service; 22.8% trade; 21.8% government; 14.4% manufacturing	**Employment:** 25.7% government; 23.4% service; 22.4% trade; 4.7% manufacturing

Fun Facts

State Date: May 29, 1848	**State Date:** July 10, 1890
Motto: Forward	**Motto:** Equal Rights
Flower: Wood Violet	**Flower:** Indian Paintbrush
Bird: Robin	**Bird:** Western Meadowlark
Tree: Sugar Maple	**Tree:** Plains Cottonwood
Song: On, Wisconsin!	**Song:** Wyoming
Nickname: Badger State	**Nicknames:** Equality State, Cowboy State
Web Site: state.wi.us	**Web Site:** state.wy.us

Source: *The World Almanac and Book of Facts 2002* (New York: World Almanac Books, 2002). **Note:** Entries under "Racial Distribution" may not add to 100% due to rounding and nonlisting of other categories. People in the Hispanic category may be any race as well as being listed separately. Population density is for land area only.

A

adapt to change to fit new conditions

African Americans descendants of people from Africa

agriculture the business of growing crops and raising animals

ancestor a relative who lived long ago

aqueduct a pipe or canal for carrying a large quantity of water

Asian Americans descendants of Asian immigrants

assembly line a process in which each worker does one part of a job before passing it on to the next worker

B

basin a bowl-shaped landform that is lower than the surrounding land

bayou a stream that flows through a swamp

bill a proposal for a new law

border a boundary that separates two places

C

canal a ditch dug across land to connect one waterway with another

canning preserving food by cooking and sealing it in cans or jars

canyon a deep, narrow valley with steep sides

capital a city where the government of a country or state is located

cave a natural underground hole

cavern a large cave

coastal plain low, flat land that runs along a coast

combine a machine pulled by horses for cutting and threshing grain

conservation the careful use of a resource

constitution a written statement of a plan for government

Constitution the plan of government for the U.S.

D

dam a wall built across a river to stop the flow of water

delta a triangle-shaped area of land at the end of a river

democracy a form of government in which people vote for their laws and leaders

desert an area of land that receives very little rain

drought a time when little or no rain falls

E

economist a social scientist who studies the economy of a community

economy the way people in a community use resources to meet their needs and wants

European Americans descendants of immigrants from Europe

executive branch the part of government that enforces laws

expedition a journey with a purpose

F

fertile soil able to produce good crops

fertilizer a substance added to soil to improve plant growth

flail a tool for beating harvested grain

floodplain low, flat land along a river that may be underwater during a flood

foothills a hilly region at the base of a mountain range

frontier the beginning of unexplored land

furrow a groove made in the soil for planting seeds

G

geographer a social scientist who studies the natural and constructed features of Earth's surface

geyser a hot spring that throws jets of heated water and steam into the air

global grid the grid formed by crisscrossing lines of latitude and longitude on a map

gorge a deep, narrow valley

H

habitat the place where an animal lives in nature

historian a social scientist who studies the past

hurricane a storm with heavy rains and high winds

I

immigrant a person who comes to live in a country from another place

inland an area of land that does not border an ocean

J

jazz a kind of music

judicial branch the part of government that settles disagreements about laws

L

Latinos people living in the United States whose ancestors were Spanish settlers

legislative branch the part of government that writes laws

lines of latitude imaginary lines around the globe that run east and west; also called *parallels*

lines of longitude imaginary lines around the globe that run between the North and South Poles; also called *meridians*

livestock animals raised on farms, such as cattle

lock elevator used to raise and lower boats

M

map key an explanation of what the symbols on a map stand for

mass production a way of making large quantities of the same product

meatpacking the preparing of meat for sale

mesa a flat-topped hill

mineral a natural material found in rock

mint a factory where coins are made

mission a Spanish settlement in the United States for teaching Christianity

Mormons members of the Church of Jesus Christ of Latter-day Saints

N

Native Americans the first Americans

navigable deep and wide enough for ships

O

oasis a place in the desert that has water

P

pass a route across mountains

peak the top of a mountain

pesticide a substance used on crops to kill insects and other pests

petroleum a thick, black, oily liquid found underground

plantation a large farm

plateau a high, flat landform that rises steeply from the land around it

political scientist a social scientist who studies government

pollution any substance that makes air, water, or soil dirty or unsafe to use

population density a measure of how many people live in one area

population map a map showing where people live in a region or an area

prairie flat or gently rolling land that is covered with grasses and wildflowers

R

reaper a machine for cutting grain

rebellion an armed fight against a government

reservation land set aside for Native Americans

reservoir an area where water is stored

revolution the overthrow of a system of government

river basin the area around a river and its tributaries

S

sawmill a factory where logs are turned into lumber

scale a diagram that explains distances on a map

scythe a curved knife on a long handle used for cutting grain

segregation separation of people because of race

self-sufficient doing everything necessary to take care of yourself

skyscraper a very tall building

social sciences the study of how people live in groups

social scientist a person who studies how people live in groups

sod a mixture of dirt and roots of grass used to build sod houses

specialty map a map that shows just one kind of information, such as rainfall or elevation

strip mine a place where minerals are scraped from the surface of the ground

swamp a low area of land that is covered by water at least part of the year

T

technology the use of tools and ideas to meet people's needs

thresh to separate grain seeds from the rest of the plant

tidewater low-lying land along the coast

transportation hub a city that serves as a center for moving goods and people

W

wastewater water that has been used

Credits

Contents